BREAKING GROUND

How Jackie Robinson Changed Brooklyn

BREAKING GROUND

How Jackie Robinson Changed Brooklyn

ALAN LELCHUK

[M]

Mandel Vilar Press

This book is typeset in Monotype Walbaum. The paper used in this book meets the minimum requirements of ANSI/NISO Z39.48-1992 (R1997). ∞

Publisher's Cataloging-In-Publication Data
Lelchuk, Alan.
  Breaking ground : how Jackie Robinson changed Brooklyn / Alan Lelchuk.
  pages ; cm
  Issued also as an ebook.
  Includes bibliographical references.
  ISBN: 978-1-942134-07-7
    1. Lelchuk, Alan. 2. Robinson, Jackie, 1919–1972—Influence. 3. Authors, American—20th century—Biography. 4. Baseball fans—New York (State)—New York—Biography. 5. Immigrant families—New York (State)—New York—History—20th century. 6. Brooklyn (New York, N.Y.)—Race relations—History—20th century. 7. Baseball—Social aspects—New York (State)—New York—History—20th century. I. Title.
PS3562.E464 Z46 2015
813/.54

Printed in the United States of America
15 16 17 18 19 20 21 22 23 / 9 8 7 6 5 4 3 2 1

Mandel Vilar Press
19 Oxford Court, Simsbury, Connecticut 06070
www.americasforconservation.org | www.mvpress.org

Dedicated to Flora Leow Natapoff, who was taken to Ebbets Field as a young girl of nine by her father in order to see Jackie play, and Judy Borodovko Walzer, who watched her baseball from the bleachers at Yankee Stadium.

Also dedicated to my sons, Saul and Daniel, who would have loved watching Jackie play.

"Keep True to the Dreams of Thy Youth."

HERMAN MELVILLE'S MOTTO

An Introduction

On July 28, 2009, at Fenway Park, the Boston Red Sox hosted a special night to retire the number of Jim Rice, their former left fielder, who had just been inducted into the Baseball Hall of Fame. In his opening remarks, Rice, standing on the twilight field, took the occasion to thank first Jackie Robinson, who, he said, "had paved the way for all black players like myself to enter the major leagues." This personal remembrance came approximately sixty-two years after Jackie first walked onto Ebbets Field in Brooklyn, April 9, 1947. The sold-out Fenway crowd of 38,000 gave that special homage to Jackie a standing ovation. Previously, Jackie had also been commemorated by the retirement of his number, 42, which had been put up on the right-field façade as a memorial to him; it was the only number that was not a Red Sox player's to be honored that way.

The splendid irony here was that Jackie actually had had a tryout with the Red Sox in Fenway Park a few years *before* Branch Rickey signed him in 1945 for Montreal, the Dodgers' farm club. But he was turned away—along with two other black players—by the southern owner of the team, Tom Yawkey, a patrician bigot who never won anything but managed to keep the Sox team all white later than any other club in the American League. So here in 2009 Jackie was memorialized on the hallowed grounds of Fenway Park, a park built from the same template as Ebbets Field, that sacred temple that long ago had been demolished in Brooklyn. The legacy of Jackie was thus extended to the retirement night of Jim Rice of the Sox, the first black player ever honored by the Red Sox. Most fitting, then, for Jim to remember Jackie.

It is also noteworthy that at the All-Star Game in 2008 there was a similar ceremony honoring Jackie, in which every ballplayer wore Jackie's number, 42, on his sleeve. This was a kind of repeat of 1997, when the fiftieth anniversary of Jackie was celebrated at all the ballparks. There have been dozens of great baseball players during the one hundred-plus years of the major leagues—Cy Young, Babe Ruth, Ty Cobb, Lou Gehrig, Joe DiMaggio, Willie Mays, Mickey Mantle, Hank Aaron, and others—but there have never been so many services honoring and commemorating them. Furthermore, the number 42 has been hoisted onto scoreboards around the league, in homage.

Why? Because Robinson did something *for and through* baseball that no other great player had ever done. Not Ruth, not Cobb, not DiMaggio, not even Mays or Aaron. In part because of the era and Branch Rickey (Robinson's mentor), in part because of his own special skills and complex character, in great part because of the tests and tribulations he endured, Jackie broke new baseball ground; he also shattered the color barrier and thereby changed the sport. And gradually, over a period of a year or more, he broke through another deeper barrier—a psychological perception in the collective consciousness of American society that stained and dishonored the image of the black man. He changed that image too. Before Rosa Parks, before Martin Luther King, before civil rights legislation and Black Power, before Barack Obama, there was Jackie. He arrived, broke the ground, and prepared it. Through baseball—then the national pastime—Robinson changed a nation profoundly.

And he instilled a stronger moral fiber in America, made it take a tougher, more honest gaze at itself. Altered our history, and laid the foundation for creating a future history. Yes, a baseball player.

After Jackie was inaugurated into the Baseball Hall of Fame (on January 23, 1962), and a party was arranged at the Waldorf Astoria Hotel in New York, here is what Martin Luther King Jr. had to say about Jackie's controversial speaking out about politics and civil rights in the five years since he had retired from playing: "He has the right . . . because back in the days when integration wasn't fashionable, he underwent the trauma and the humiliation and the loneliness which comes with being a pilgrim walking the lonesome byways toward the high road of Freedom. He was a sit-inner before there were sit-ins, a freedom rider before freedom rides. And that is why we honor him tonight" (Testimonial Dinner, July 20, 1962).

This small book is about those heady and radical changes, how they looked and felt, how they came about, and how one person, myself, witnessed it all, first as a young boy and fan, and later, as a mature citizen of the republic.

This is also a book about how a borough of New York City, Brooklyn, known back then in America as a comic town (through baseball and movies), greeted Jackie, grew with him, adopted him, celebrated him. That first summer, fans and citizens around the country watched with increasing interest. What was viewed early on as a mere sports story by the dismissive *New York Times*, which relegated the story to the back pages of the sports section, quickly became a riveting subject for the nation. And Brooklyn was at the center of the story as much as Jackie. It was not an accident that Branch Rickey, the wise general manager of the Dodgers who brought Jackie into baseball, decided to venture his great gamble in the Borough of Kings. With a population of nearly three million by 1947, it was a town of great diversity, and many immigrants. Those citizens of Brooklyn, especially the young like myself, were the pioneering audience, and jury, for Jackie. If the experiment succeeded here, it would succeed across the river and elsewhere across the land.

So, Jackie was teamed up with Brooklyn, a hero and his setting— maybe like Babe Ruth and the Bronx, or Pushkin and Moscow. And actually, Jackie had some of both in him: the unlikely baseball god and the great poet, half-Negro, of Russia. And why shouldn't the unique baseball player who became a central figure in the great American tapestry be associated with such diverse figures of literary history? Isn't his tale one of poetry and mythology mingled with native history to create a fabled and enduring legend for a people, a country? How else to explain his force, his fight, his iconic status?

I met Jackie twice, both times for his autograph, outside Ebbets Field. I was nine years old, and I waited for him outside the players' exit with my scorecard. The first time, he was walking with a small group of players, and after getting a few autographs, from Hermanski, Roe, Reese, I asked for his. He signed it in a small legible handwriting, on my scorecard, and looked at me, asking my name. It was a brief meeting, a few minutes, as the others were waiting up ahead. The second meeting was longer, as I caught him walking alone, carrying his bag, wearing his tan raincoat, and he stared at me, remembering. "You're Alan," he said, in his gravelly voice, and I nodded, surprised. He continued to peer at me, his handsome ebony face probing, and he said something like, "What do you want to be when you grow up?" I responded, "A baseball player." I smiled. "But really, a writer of books." "What sort?" "Oh, maybe a sportswriter, or maybe a writer of adventure books." He nodded, scribbled his greeting, handed it to me, and, putting his hand on my shoulder, said, "Stay on course." As he studied my face, I felt his sudden intensity, as though he were gazing inside of me, to see what I was made of, maybe like a scientist who was studying a specimen to make sure he wasn't missing something. Then his somber gaze softened, he gave me a small smile, and I steadied myself from shaking.

It was a meeting to remember—I was a boy of nine, and he a famous ballplayer of twenty-seven—and it stayed with me, through the years of college and graduate school and starting a career as a writer; and I came to feel, years later, that that meeting resembled the *Great Expectations* opening, in the marshes between the boy Pip and the ex-convict Magwitch, that outlaw who eventually becomes the boy's secret benefactor. In certain ways, Jackie came to fulfill that role in my own life, as a furtive benefactor in ways both spiritual and aesthetic. So this little book is also a personal testament to his long shadow and influence upon that young boy, and this older man.

For after all, there have been so many books written about Jackie, by sportswriters, historians, social critics. Perhaps it is only—or especially—through a personal perspective that the often-told narrative can be enhanced and brought back alive. My hope is that Jackie would find himself vividly portrayed and felt here, in this account of the way it happened for me back then. Such personal witnessing and authentic experiencing should also appeal to the general reader, as well as the scholar, fan, student of history, or old Brooklynite.

The Brooklyn Project

Overleaf: Consuelo Kanaga
(American, 1894–1978). [Untitled]
(Tenements, New York), mid–late
1930s. Toned gelatin silver
photograph, 9½ x 7¼ in. (24.1 x 18.4 cm).
Credit: Brooklyn Museum, Gift of
Wallace B. Putnam from the estate of
Consuelo Kanaga, 82.65.38

In the beginning, that spring of 1947, there were three basic colors, you could say (and see): the bright green of the diamond field, the white of the baseball players (all fifty) and umpires and fans, and the ebony of the single Negro player. That's how it looked; that's how it was. Everyone on the green rural field in the middle of Brooklyn in April 1947 was white, with the exception of the stocky black player who had come in from Montreal to play with the Dodgers. The testing of whether the all-white major leagues, with about 350 players, was going to allow a Negro to play through the season would begin then and last through the whole six-month season of 1947. It was a test of epic social and moral proportions, equal in its way for our nation to the atomic testing of a few years before, in Los Alamos, New Mexico, of the bomb, which would change the nature of warfare and destruction. A human experiment, in contrast to the Manhattan Project, this Brooklyn Project would change the nature of race relations in America.

Let's start with this question: What did baseball mean for the country in the days of post–World War II America? Unlike now, when football has overtaken it in terms of mass popularity, baseball then was the main game in town, the national pastime, the turf of American dreams. (Horseracing and boxing were next in line.) We were coming out of a momentous war, our last war of clearly justified patriotism, maybe even a war of survival, and we had won; the nation, which had been wounded and tested, was recovering strongly, prospering, and hopeful. The mood was upbeat everywhere. That buoyantly upward spirit pervaded all areas of our national life, from public to private, especially with the economy booming. The golden age of our national power and prosperity was a major fact around the world. Though the Cold War had started, we were plenty strong enough to feel confident in the international arena; but where uncertainty lurked—or loomed?—was in our collective consciousness, our domestic life. Who we really were, our fullest identity, was a serious question.

While we were made aware daily of our fight against Communism, we also became painfully and increasingly aware of our political fight against McCarthyism and its melodramatic forms of fake, dogmatic patriotism, its deliberate scaremongering jingoism. A growing number of people acknowledged this developing political rift in our midst. But what we were less aware of—or less willing to be aware of—was our deeper battle, the struggle of the races. Negroes were not only second-class citizens, but in many parts of the country they were barely visible as men and women. Half real, half mirage, they served as public entertainers on stage or in movies, and as porters, busboys, shoeshine boys, in our daily life for the most part. It is not surprising that the most important book about the race war was not written by an American, but by a Swedish sociologist, Gunnar Myrdal, in 1944, *An American Dilemma*. Obviously, our own consciousness of race was a dilemma, an unwanted dilemma.

My own connection with much of that turbulence was rather personal, in different ways. First, as a keen baseball fan at ages eight and nine in 1940s Brooklyn; second, as a young friend of Burt Bream, a twenty-three-year-old Air Force veteran who lived in our Brownsville apartment building; and third, as the son of a Russian immigrant and fellow-traveler Communist who cared little about baseball, until Jackie came along. Burt was my adopted big brother before he went off to the war as a navigator in a B-17. He was shot down over Germany, became a prisoner of war, was shot again as he escaped, and returned home, eventually to have a series of surgeries for shards of glass bullets in his body. In between hospital tours, he was a free young man; and since Jackie had just come to town, Burt was delighted to chart regular visits to Ebbets Field, taking me along, to see the Dodgers and their unique new player. Since he wore his first lieutenant's uniform, we were invited free through the turnstiles; and since he also bore a Purple Heart along with his other medals, we were quickly waved down by an usher from the lower grandstand to box seats behind first base, maybe seventy-five feet from Robinson, where he played that first year. Being a wounded war veteran counted for a lot in those days—the best box seats by the field for free, just up from the Dodgers' dugout. The native spoils of war extended graciously to myself, a nine-year-old fourth grader, and already a veteran Brooklyn fan.

Jackie's bright ebony color stood out immediately, as I said, in the sea of whiteness of the Dodgers players in their blue and white uniforms. It was strange, like seeing a Masai warrior set down on the wrong movie set, or Bigger Thomas from Wright's *Native Son* trotting out onto the field, mistaking his *fictional home ground* for this Brooklyn baseball turf, in front of amazed baseball players. How could that happen? Had he entered the wrong sport or a mistaken scenario? When you were sitting there, in the lower stands close to the field, it was an odd feeling, a jazz riff suddenly running in the midst of a classical composition.

What else stood out in that first month or two of games, against the Braves, the Giants, and the Phillies, were two things: the level of his play and the level of hostility he faced. Jackie could field, hit, throw, and run; oh, could he run. Or rather, he reinvented base running, it may be said, made it over into a kind of art form. On the bases, Jackie was a dark outlaw, a brazen creature, and there were few if any before or after who performed his base path *adventures*. He wasn't the swiftest, but he was the smartest; not the fastest, but the most daring. And once he got to know the opposing players and pitchers, he grew shrewder and even more daring. (The last really dangerous runner had been the "Georgia Peach," Ty Cobb, back in 1910–20, who was more famous—or infamous—for his lethal spikes and mean intentions.) Jackie was developing his own style, a sort of one-man guerrilla strategy of attacking, physically and mentally, the traditional defenses of the opposing team. Uniquely surprising for baseball.

There was something else that was surprising right off: he didn't look like a great athlete—although he had been a star in three sports in college: football, basketball, field and track—or even a special baseball player. Not tall and strong and muscular, with great upper body strength, sinewy, etc. No, not at all. He had sloping shoulders, walked pigeon-toed, looked as though he was in constant pain, and seemed to have no limberness in his gait. Was the problem his age? At twenty-seven, he was already old for a rookie. Maybe the wrong Robinson had turned up? (A fitting parallel to another non-athletic-looking player, a pudgy fellow who had a funny pear shape and spindly legs, a cocky kid from a Baltimore orphanage who was to become the greatest slugger, and player, in baseball history. Such is the nature of the old native game—that it doesn't demand a great height or huge weight to make for greatness.) And when he stepped to the plate, this Jackie had a most awkward stance that made you wonder how he was going to hit the ball. His bat was held way too high, cocked way up behind his body, making you doubt that he could bring it down and through quickly enough to connect with the major league fastballs or the dropping curves. Was this *the athlete* who was going to show us new ways of dramatic winning? The Negro Moses who would lead our Dodgers out from their long history of futility and comedy?

You have to understand the excitement generated by Jackie in the neighborhood and among us kids. The first Negro player coming to our league was coming to our team, via Mr. Rickey. This was a great event happening, like Tom Mix from the radio drama riding in. You could feel the charge in the schools, the schoolyards, the playgrounds, the corner hangouts. No need for Twitter or e-mails or Facebook to feel the electricity powering. We had the radio voice of Red Barber and the six major newspapers with the dense sports sections, and word of mouth in the luncheonettes, the subways, the trolley cars. Even the local merchants in my Brownsville/East Flatbush shops would chat with me about it—at the fresh fish and smoked salmon (lox) shop downstairs on Sutter Avenue (where white fish trucked in overnight from the Great Lakes sold for twelve cents), or the jewelry shop run by an English Jewish jeweler and his spinster sister who served me afternoon tea when I was eight; they all wanted to know about the new News of the Day, Jackie. Who was this creature?

Further evidence of his spreading power came from my Hebrew school, the Sholem Aleichem Bund school, which I attended in the late afternoons after my regular school day. One 4 p.m. I was looking furtively at a story I had clipped from the *New York Post* with a photograph of Jackie sliding, which I buried beneath my Yiddish story collection on the small, slanted wooden school desk. When I was suddenly called upon to read aloud from a Singer tale and interpret, I was caught off guard and mumbled, unusual for me. Swiftly my teacher, Lehrer Goichberg, a vigorous man of fifty who had concentration camp numbers on his forearm, approached the desk, ready to grab my arm and forcefully discover the source of my confusion and toss it away. When he saw the photo and story of Jackie, his face changed; he stopped in his tracks, advised me quietly this was not the time for that, but, with a sudden smile, he asked, "Nu, do you think he will make it, *kinde?*" I nodded slowly, stared at his lined serious face, and felt a surge in my heart for the teacher, who had kept up with the new Brooklyn excitement.

Even in my father's social club on Topscott Street, a leftover from the old World War II air raid wardens' storefront, the immigrant gab on Sundays, sailing through pinochle and chess and cigar smoke, was about Jackie coming to play here in Brooklyn, instead of Truman's policies or the Cold War. I was taken there on Sunday mornings, dressed up in my formal woolen knickers suit at my father's direction, to show off my chess ability, which he had nurtured. Before we traveled uptown to see some Russian or Chaplin movies on Fourteenth Street at the Stanley Theater, I was able to serve as a kind of translator/guide to the higher standards and sweetness of baseball for those greenhorn East European immigrants.

In 1946 Bill Veeck, the baseball entrepreneur who was negotiating to buy the Cleveland Indians and wanted to obtain a black player for integration, wrote, "I moved slowly and carefully, perhaps even timidly. It is usually overlooked, but if Jackie Robinson was the ideal man to break the color barrier, Brooklyn was also the ideal place. I wasn't sure about Cleveland." Veeck was right on. Brooklyn was the right place for such a baseball—and social and moral—revolution. It was a burgeoning town whose population had grown from one and a half million (1,666,000) in 1900 to nearly three million (2,738,000) in 1950. (A borough that was the fifth biggest city in America!) Brooklyn 1947 was not a town of expensive condo or townhouse owners, out-of-towners in artist lofts, Park Slope yuppies, or white-collar professionals deserting Manhattan. It didn't have gentrified neighborhoods or gentrified authors, pretty people or pop tunes; it wasn't known for its charm or graciousness. (Although the 1945 *A Tree Grows in Brooklyn* sought charm.) But we, on the inside, savored its delights: Dutch-planted trees and tulips, parks galore, sandy beaches with Atlantic waves and long boardwalks, superior public libraries and public high schools, Olmstead and Vaux boulevards and parks. For that pair of America's foremost landscape designers, Prospect Park was their very best.

Yet the old 1940s–50s Brooklyn was also a tough town, a mongrel site of distinct, discrete neighborhoods, where you had to know the turf before you journeyed there, lest a local gang—Black Hats, The Syndicate, or Syndicate Midgets—would suddenly encircle, interrogate, bully you. (Maybe flip open a five-inch switchblade for show-and-tell.) A town where East New York street smarts or the Brownsville School of Hard Knocks counted for more than Flatbush credentials or Ivy League college degrees. Where Bugsy Siegel, Louis "Lepke" Buchalter, Meyer Lansky had all honed their gangster trade—before taking it national—and still haunted the history and streets. (For example, my Bar Mitzvah was in a small shul down Strauss Street from where Bugsy was known to have sliced the throats of difficult clients getting their barbershop haircuts.) Yet a few hundred steps away in East New York was the Palace Theater, where the best of Yiddish theater was performed—plays by Sholem Asch, I. B. Singer, I. L. Peretz; actors like Menashe Skulnik, Leo Fuchs. Those were streets of diverse surprises, and often might lead to private encounters with ghosts from a recent legendary past.

Moreover, it was a city of immigrants who came from all over: Holland first, then Poland and Russia, Naples and Sicily, Ireland and Germany, and even Scandanavia. Those ethnic groups, like the Negroes, formed their own neighborhoods, imitating the old country; they were hard working, fighting upward, each with particular skills and hopes. They stayed mostly unto their own habits, families, and churches or synagogues. If there came to be a single majority, it was the Jews; by 1950 one in three immigrants was Jewish. A huge fact. There was, however, no one great leader or inspiring figure for the whole town—Walt Whitman had lived a century earlier, and George Gershwin was decades before—like Manhattan had with its charismatic Mayor Fiorello LaGuardia, or the Bronx with Joltin' Joe DiMaggio, both New York and national figures.

And as newcomers, Brooklyn's folks were still looking in on America from the outside. They were fond of their comic Dodgers. My father's generation of immigrants were outsiders, at best (humorous) second-class citizens, unrefined souls—especially alongside the comfortable, more refined ladies and gentlemen of Manhattan. But below best, they were greenhorn misfits mocked for their Polish or Russian accents, insecure citizens still scrambling about for their place in a permanent home. (See Henry James on the "motley" crew of Jews he witnessed on the Lower East Side.) As outsiders, they were ready and waiting, it may be said, to accept a symbolic outsider, to embrace him as one of their own, and to make him over, psychologically, into a folk hero. Did they know, or could anyone know, what or who that creature would be—a politician, a writer, a lawyer? Maybe only Branch Rickey had a hint of it. (As Bill Veeck had had?) No, that folk hero would not—and could not—be one of their own, one with old European roots, but rather a different sort of outsider in every way. But who would have dreamed that he would be a native Negro, a baseball player from a faraway land called California, and that that fellow would become a permanent and honorary citizen of Brooklyn?

Inevitably, then, when Jackie became instrumental in helping our "Bums" win the pennant in his very first year, he became our man, our adopted folk hero. How ironic then, that ten years later, when the Dodgers were yanked away from Brooklyn by a new, greedy owner in 1957 to go west to Southern California, where Jackie grew up, he refused to go. *Brooklyn was his home now*, he declared in a solitary but firm voice, and the only authentic Dodgers team that he wanted to play for had the name of Brooklyn—not Los Angeles—attached to it. Once again Jackie played the rebel, and remained the Brooklyn hero. And in staying put on his adopted home ground, refusing to move on from his Brooklyn turf, he displayed a Bartleby-like free will, refusing to move from his home ground and his high ideals, a gentleman true to his own preferences.

It was little surprise that Jackie, in the early going, didn't hit well, in fact was in a sharp batting slump, going 0 for 20 at bats in his first five games. (Compare Willie Mays in 1951, going 0 for 25 in his first six games.) First and obvious was the pressure on him to do well, having been promoted suddenly to the parent squad, replacing the regular first baseman, Ed Stevens. Beyond that, however, there were two other reasons. He started out with a bruised shoulder, and he was playing in a brand new position, first base. Throughout his career, in Kansas City and Montreal, he had been a second baseman or shortstop; but in Brooklyn, Eddie Stanky was a fixture at second, so Jackie was asked, suddenly in late spring training, to play first, because Rickey wanted him in the lineup, knowing he was a superior athlete and what an immediate draw he'd be. So Jackie had to learn this new position on the fly. Supposedly, according to the newspapers, he was in jeopardy of losing his job early on; and even, as he acknowledged in his autobiography written just after that first year, *Jackie Robinson: My Own Story*, privately depressed. (It should be noted that in his first year in organized baseball, playing for Montreal in the International League, he was advised to take off for several August days by his manager, Clay Hopper, who saw that Jackie was suffering under great tension and pressure. Jackie took off for four or five games and confidentially went to see a doctor, who saw he needed rest, badly. Clearly the nervous exhaustion was right there beneath the surface, and could have easily led to a breakdown.)

In a way, this down time in his early play allowed the fans time to look him over carefully, as it were, and to consider what was going on. Of course hostility was going on, at different levels, along with fear, fury, strangeness, and fascination; it was like suddenly spotting a Kafkaesque Bug wearing the number 42 and lumbering onto the field in a Dodgers Blue (uniform). The experience was strange, bizarre, and you could sense the surrealism. Would the Bug hold up mentally to all the pressures put upon him? And what about physically, when teams like the Phillies and the Cardinals would come to town with their many southern and openly racist players? Could the strange creature make it intact through a whole season and not break down in mind or body? Or would he/it be stomped upon, spiked, and squeezed out of his/its vile life?

This dire prospect was what the Prospero of Ebbets Field, Branch Rickey, had carefully prepared and planned for when he picked Jackie to be the first Negro to cross over the taboo color line of baseball segregation. Rickey, a small-town Midwesterner but a worldly man of parts, a rotund man wearing odd hats and wire-rim spectacles and bow ties, had been a shrewd lawyer and businessman, an instructor of Latin, and a sharp evaluator of baseball talent; most of all, he was a bold and gutsy citizen. He had worked in the major leagues for many years, in all sorts of jobs, from coach to owner to manager, winding up as a general manager of the weak Cardinals. He started at the bottom by creating the first farm system for that team—and for all of baseball—that is, the minor leagues, where youngsters learned the fundamentals of the game and progressed upward gradually, from Class A to Double and Triple AAA; he made the Cards an outstanding team by the time he left them. He knew and loved all aspects of baseball, and believed in constant instruction and refinement of skills. In 1914, at the start of his managing career, a sportswriter said this about him: "He is a Professor of Baseball. His efficiency courses in sliding, base running, and batting mark a new departure in the game." Rickey, himself unique, came to admire and appreciate Jackie's unique skills.

Branch Rickey came to Brooklyn in 1944, serving as general manager and president of baseball operations, taking over a team of perennial also-rans that had never won the World Series. In fact the Dodgers were famous for their comic interludes—two runners tagged out at home plate on the same play, mishandling a third strike to close out the ninth inning of a World Series game against the Yankees, and turning sure victory into stunning defeat—and for constantly playing in the shadow of the perennial champions from across the river, the almighty Yankees. "Mr. Rickey"—what everyone seemed to call him—knew the history, the context, the challenges. Ambitiously, he wanted three things with his new club: making the Dodgers profitable, winning a pennant and a World Series, and changing baseball. (And maybe, transforming the nation?) A simple plan, you could say.

To be sure, Mr. Rickey had been searching for several years for the right colored ballplayer to help accomplish at least two, and maybe three, of his missions. He knew that the right Negro would excite and draw the fans—both the untapped Negro population and the whole baseball audience—making the Dodgers more profitable; help the Bums win a World Series and give the team and the borough an elevated status; and also, change history, not merely baseball history but American history. A tall agenda. Where, one will ask, did Rickey's passion come from for this perilous journey? In his autobiography, he described a situation in his younger days as a manager of the Ohio Wesleyan college team, when he came back to his hotel room and found his young black player, Charles Thomas, crying in the bathroom while washing his hands, desperately trying to wash the blackness or peel the skin off his flesh ("Damned skin . . . damned skin! If only I could rub it off!") because his stain of color had kept the team from hotel housing in a segregated town. Rickey claimed that moment as a turning point for him, haunting him throughout his mature life, and he swore one day he would make up for that young man's racial anguish, and seek to integrate the playing field of organized baseball. That crucial memory stamped itself upon him, as he wrote, and drove him relentlessly. Did we know then that the avuncular looking man with the bow tie and infectious smile was on his own compulsive mission?

Mr. Rickey had sent his Brooklyn scouts searching for a player who possessed just the right combination of baseball skills and character traits, some of which would mirror his own: A player of formidable mental and physical skills. A college educated Negro who could understand what the stakes were and not be daunted. A fellow who burned with passion on the inside, but could manage to stay cool and restrained on the outside. A strong-willed figure, maybe even a fiery rebel, sure, but also a calculating one, who could measure the risks and rewards of the struggle at hand, and act for the good of the team and the ultimate Cause—breaking the race boundary in major league baseball, the country's national pastime and passion—and not himself. A player and a man who could stick it out, on the field and off, for a sustained period of time—a whole summer and fall (of the game) and beyond—a fellow of uncommon mental stamina as well as physical skill. In Jackie's biography as Mr. Rickey knew it—and in the year-long scouting reports of super scout Clyde Sukeforth, the former Maine blueberry farmer who had been following closely Jackie's career— he saw those commingled and complex traits and characteristics.

All those traits had to be proven out in a private interview that Mr. Rickey conducted with Jackie in October 1945, at the Dodgers offices on Montague Street in Brooklyn. There, with friend Sukeforth in the room, Mr. Rickey explained what he was looking for, questioned Jack in a gentlemanly way, and asked him various questions, sizing him up. Jackie answered politely enough, believing that this white general manager was interviewing him for a place in a new Negro league to be started. He was shocked to discover that Rickey was interviewing him for a spot with the Montreal farm team, and then maybe with the real Dodgers. ("I was thrilled, scared, and excited," Jackie remembered. "I was incredulous. Most of all, I was speechless.") After stating that he needed good ballplayers to win a pennant, Rickey then abruptly changed tone and direction, and went at the stunned Jackie with imitations of racists he would meet with in baseball—a white hotel clerk, a white waiter, a railroad conductor, and a vengeful base runner running with spikes high—and declaimed, in Jack's face, "How do you like that, nigger boy!" And swung his fist at Jackie's head! What was he going to do about it? Jackie, shocked, stood up, furious, but controlled himself, stayed silent, sat back down.

Rickey countered with, "That's exactly what you have to do, Jack, turn your other cheek, and for this whole season. Can you do that? Because there are going to be worse names and harsher insults you will have to take, and *do nothing*. Just turn the other cheek. Can you do that for a whole year?" Jackie took a minute to understand fully what he was being asked to endure, and slowly nodded, and replied that he understood, he could do it. Supposedly, Rickey then handed Jack a copy of a popular book, *The Story of Christ*, and pointed to the passage in what the author, Giovanni Papini, called the "most stupefying of His revolutionary teachings," where turning the other cheek is given the higher value over an "eye for an eye, tooth for a tooth." The one good Methodist (Rickey) gave the other good Methodist (Jackie) the best evidence of the necessity for a total "turn the other cheek" nonviolent approach.

The now-famous interview, corroborated by Jackie in his autobiography (and detailed by his biographer Rampersad), convinced Rickey he had chosen the right man. He signed Jack immediately to a private contract, kept secret from everyone, including Jackie's family, for several weeks, until the official Montreal signing. Can we imagine Jackie upon leaving that office after those two stunning hours? Hardly. The terms of his contract were $3,500 bonus, $600 per month, to play in Montreal, the highest Dodgers farm team, where Rickey knew that Jackie would be treated well by the proud French Canadian fans. News of this interview leaked out to us, though Brooklyn had already felt something in the air, a signaling, and even if it was rumors at first, we were excited. Columnists, like Jimmy Cannon in the *Post* and Dick Young in the *Daily*

Mirror, murmured tips. (Not to mention the most prominent follower of the story, Lester Rodney of the *Daily Worker*, the Communist newspaper my father read on occasion.) Something big was happening, though we didn't know precisely what it was. Or that the great trial was beginning.

Mr. Rickey appeared, to my mind, as a kind of sporting extension of FDR, who had died in spring 1945; they both were gentlemanly, genial, practical, but also shrewd, wise, and visionary, keenly interested in the good of the whole community, not merely a special interest. Both had a vision of history and a passionate belief in American justice. Both were fighters too, but always in a careful and strategic way. Though obviously they were an odd and incongruous pairing, for me as a boy of nine in Brooklyn, those two were the grand heroes of the nation. Soon enough, Jackie was to join them in my boyhood pantheon. FDR, Rickey, Robinson—a Brooklyn boy's Holy Trinity.

(If the voice here is sometimes that of a boy, it is only partly by design, and partly by the power of that boy's feelings still beating strongly in the adult, remembering here. Without that voice, in certain moments, I fear that the *true felt experience* of those days would be changed into something merely academic, if not forfeited.)

Apart from Rickey and Jackie, there were two other key protagonists in this colossal American drama, played out on the unlikely stage of a sporting field. The first was a radio announcer. Red Barber broadcast the Dodgers games on WHN throughout New York City, at a time when radio was *the* medium for spreading the news and sports, and giving firsthand impressions, with television sets few and far between. A true blue southerner, born in Mississippi and raised in Florida, Red Barber had a deep southern drawl, employed homespun country phrases in his baseball descriptions, and had developed into the trusted, and beloved, Voice of the team. What he said, how he said it, and how he viewed things, counted for a lot with the citizen-fans of the borough. (Old Gold Cigarettes stayed a favorite sponsor because of Red.) His country phrases were memorable, if somewhat mysterious, such as, "We got a rhubarb growin' in the infield" (a dispute with the umps); "sittin' up here in the catbird seat" (in the announcer's booth); "the bases are FOB" (full of Brooklyns). Or an infielder "tearin' up the pea patches" (going on a rampage) and "walkin' in tall cotton" (doing very well). Or, about the Cards' smooth short-stop, Marty Marion, "He's out there at shortstop, movin' easy as a bank of fog" (moving gracefully). It was through Red's quiet rhe-torical eloquence and rural witty sensibility that we city boys learned how the new Negro ballplayer was doing. (Decades later, it was through Bob Edwards' weekly interviews with Red on NPR's Morning Edition that we learned more about how difficult the situation was from Red's point of view, as he was going through his own personal trial by fire. After all, Negroes had been "dark-ies" and shadows in his Florida growing up.) Interestingly enough, at the very end of Jackie's 1948 autobiography, in his "salute" page, he acknowledged the part that Red (and his assistant host) had played in his first year: "And last, but not least, I want to express my gratitude to Red Barber and Connie Desmond, the radio announcers of all Dodgers games." Was that the first—and the last—time that a sporting star acknowledged the help and support of a radio announcer?

The fourth "protagonist" in this developing national drama was the Kings County borough of Brooklyn—its citizens and its home office and unofficial church, Ebbets Field. Let's start with the borough, a wilderness area across the East River populated by the Dutch back in the 1600s; they created the first village

("Breucklyn") and planted trees, tulips, and green parks in that sparse rural backwater. Through the years, the town began to develop a reputation as a cozy place for newcomer families and small merchants, churches and synagogues, and the newer immigrants, most from Europe. Home to a burgeoning population of nearly three million by the end of World War II, Brooklyn was larger than most of our cities. It grew into the largest borough of the five, and was a good place to visit for its sandy beaches and Atlantic ocean swimming and deep sea fishing (on days off, Dodgers players used to go over to Sheepshead Bay to go out for bluefish); for its Coney Island playground of steeplechase rides and rousing amusements; and for its long handsome parkways like Kings Highway and Eastern Parkway (designed by Olmstead and Vaux). The borough also took pride in its first-class Botanical Gardens, its superb public library and adjacent, elegant Prospect Park (Olmstead again), and in its famously comical, losing baseball team and cozy baseball field, built by Charlie Hercules Ebbets in 1913. Despite these attractions, however, it remained a quaint side attraction, a quiet town across the river from the noisy main-tent glamour of international Manhattan, that vertical colossus at the other end of the Brooklyn Bridge.

Dostoevski once wrote that each unique city, like St. Petersburg, had its own special destiny, and Brooklyn became a Dostoevskian case in point. That is, with the coming of Jackie Robinson to the Dodgers, the quiet side attraction took a different turn, a major turn towards the center of attention. The cozy family town, a conglomerate of discrete neighborhoods, each the site of a different population—Jewish, Negro, Irish, Italian—was suddenly acquiring a new purposefulness. Would Brooklyn be the memorable site of success of this radical human experiment? (Again, like Los Alamos being forever attached to our nuclear experiment.) The diverse but segregated population was being stirred and transformed by the alchemy of a baseball rookie, and something new was emerging. The town and the city sensed it, and soon the country would know it.

A new phenomenon was in town, and it—or he—was happening in the Flatbush area of Brooklyn, not on Manhattan's Broadway or Wall Street or Yankee Stadium. What its true nature was, and what the results would be of that phenomenon, were in question. But what was not in question was that Ebbets Field was the place to be; that's where the real action was. I recall sitting in the box seats and lower grandstands and seeing families with tall men in straw hats and pale suits with neckties, and blonde wives wearing pretty hats and summer dresses, obvious out-of-towners. Chatting occasionally, I learned they had come in from Kansas, Iowa, Illinois, and Nebraska, to "see the colored boy everyone was talking about" play for the Dodgers. They were interested, curious, aroused enough to take the IRT El across the river from Midtown to see him play, and take their kids too. We had become an attraction to rival the Broadway plays and Manhattan skyscrapers, the usual destinations.

Jackie was setting the Dodgers and Brooklyn on the map, and Brooklyn was feeling its oats, nurturing a new national pride, and developing a fresh soul. Newspapers from around the country were now covering the story, on and off the sporting pages, and the story would soon be major news in *Time* and *Life*. Brooklyn was acquiring its own celebrity-hood, an ambiguous one, to be sure—not a clear-cut Yankee white one exemplified by Joe DiMaggio and Mickey Mantle—and Jackie, the new semi-celebrity, was playing on a small stadium and baseball field, where you could practically touch him. Moreover, he was playing on an odd field in sporting history, one not yet clearly defined, where he was a kind of high-wire performer crossing over—or through—American history at some precarious angle. Would he fall and crash, and if so, what would that mean? Or, on the other side, what if he made it through standing and succeeded?

Ebbets Field helped, by means of its cozy dimensions and close-in stands. It was built for fans to be very near and intimate with the field and the players, very close along the right and left field sidelines—maybe fifteen or twenty feet between field and stands down the lines—so unlike most of today's modern stadiums, which are designed with acres of space between the foul lines and the fans in the stands. For players to catch foul balls, that space is a benefit; but for fans, it keeps the game and the players at a remote, cool distance. Ebbets Field—like Fenway Park in Boston or Wrigley Field in Chicago—was like a family field, where the players and the fans mingled, often exchanging words of humor and important advice! You got to know every inch of the facility, every nook and cranny, every loophole and intricacy. For example, right field held the scoreboard, but above that was a thirty-eight-foot-high chain link screen, which we kids employed for our own special benefit. The routine went this way: in batting practice one of us would climb up, on the Bedford Avenue side of the screen, and wait for a ball to be hit over it, so he could signal his partner waiting below on the street that a ball was heading over and where to race to grab it. For if you brought the baseball to the front gate, you'd get in free. So if one kid got in free, we'd split the cost of the ticket, half of sixty cents for a bleacher seat, or half of a dollar and a quarter for a grandstand. (Sometimes it bounded into the Mobil Gas Station across the way, and the fielder below would have to hustle to make sure he didn't get in trouble with a gas attendant or it didn't hit and dent a car stopping for gas.) In Ebbets Field especially, the fans were a key part of the action, a piece of the neighborhood, a strategic tenth player joining the nine playing on the fair side of the foul lines.

I often sat, in later years after Burt had married and moved to California, down by the right field line, in a grandstand seat edging the field, just where the Dodgers relief pitchers warmed up, no screen or partition separating them from us. So you might chat with them, if they wished—for example, Joe Black was a very cordial and chatty reliever—or watch them warm up, like they were playing catch in your backyard, and, from fifteen or twenty feet away, you'd observe them firing pitches and hitting the catcher's leather with a delicious thud! What a sound, so familiarly baseball-ish! (Like hearing the crack of the bat hitting the baseball, and knowing intuitively, almost like an outfielder, what sort of hit it would be, line drive or pop-up or fly ball.) In brief, the physical proximity was such that fans participated more closely and existed as an extension of the team. Close familiarity, hearing precise words of encouragement or curses, or baseball phrases of obscenity, seeing the small habits of the different players, were part and parcel of the atmosphere, which increased the devotion of us Dodgers fans. Truthfully, no religion or church could have really challenged or competed. The site itself, Ebbets Field, was too intimate and too palpable, too strongly a sacred diamond, with our summer boygods playing in their fluttering baseball uniforms. This was heaven incarnate—the boys in Dodgers blue and white playing the princely game on the country green grass, right there a stone's throw away.

But for the grand Brooklyn Project to work, changing the game—and, inevitably, changing the nation—Jackie had to prove himself baseball-wise, and he had to do it over a period of time, through a whole season (and more, after the first big test season). Baseball is a slow game, the most nuanced and complicated of games, and made especially for the thinking athlete. (Football, on the other hand, was made for the thinking coach.) Jackie, himself most complicated, was a thinking athlete. One of the smartest who ever played the game. And consider: he came to this sport later than to his other sports.

He was very good, immediately—outside of the early hitting drought—in all the areas of the game: running, throwing, fielding, baseball IQ; but clearly, he excelled in running, his kind of running. (Like saying that Astaire excelled in *his* kind of dancing, a unique style.) In running and thinking, you would want to add. Because his sense of running the bases was both intuitive and learned, like a natural-born mathematician who simply needed to learn a few formulas and basic propositions to make his way into the highest realms. Jackie had run track and long-jumped in track and field at college, run and swivel-hipped on the football gridiron, run and leaped on the basketball floor, and, for a short time, run the base paths in the Negro Leagues. Running and wreaking havoc in all sports had been his art and skill since he was a small boy in Pasadena, on the playgrounds and high school practice fields, when he had showed himself to be a winner among the older white boys, who had at first to accept him, soon chose him first for their pickup teams, and then began to recruit him for the high school and college teams. At UCLA on a track scholarship he became the leading rusher on the football team and in the Pacific-10; in broad jump as a sophomore he broke his brother Mack's NCAA record; as a walk-on to the basketball team, he became its leading scorer. Even in tennis, which he hardly ever played, he showed formidable skills. Not since Jim Thorpe, the Native American phenomenon of the 1930s who starred in every sport he played, had there been as versatile and outstanding an athlete as Jackie. And here he was running again, among the same young white lads who now were grown up a bit, and playing in the big leagues, and again he was going to have to *compel* them to accept him. It was an old challenge newly shaped and on new grounds, for the same competitive athletic genius.

A few telling events occurred. In March 1947, just as Montreal was going to play the parent Dodgers team in a pre-season game in Panama, Mr. Rickey, the paradoxically prudent yet bold impresario, suddenly wrote and advised Jackie: "I want you to get on base and run wild. Steal their pants off. Be the most conspicuous player on the field. The newspapermen from New York will send good stories back about you and help mold favorable public opinion." Especially bold advice in the face of an attempted revolt—a player petition signed right then in Panama by a group of five Dodgers, including the most popular, Dixie Walker, against playing with a Negro. (Yet Pee Wee Reese, the soft-spoken team captain from Louisville, declined, saying, "Dixie came to the room, and he asked Pete Reiser and me to sign that I wouldn't play with a black man. I looked at it, and I just flatly refused. I just said, 'Hey, look, man, I just got out of the service after three years. I don't care if this man is black, blue, or what the hell color he is. I have to play baseball. I wasn't trying to be The Great White Father. I just wanted to play ball. And Pete refused to sign it too.") Rickey quickly and decisively dismissed the petition, tearing it up in front of the group and telling them they would play or sit at home, without a job. They sulked and played. And when Dixie Walker, his best player, wrote him a note saying he was not up to the challenge, Rickey told him he would trade him, and he did, after the season.

Meanwhile, Jackie followed Rickey's sage advice. In the seven pre-season games against the Dodgers, Jackie proceeded to steal the show, "stealing their pants off," stealing seven bases in seven games and leading both clubs in hitting, at the phenomenal average of .625. The New York newspapers crowed. He was called up to the Dodgers a few weeks later, in mid-April. A potential storm had been diverted, and what could have been just another ordinary exhibition series was turned into an exhibition of Robinson's excellence. What a turn of events.

It should be said that we in Brooklyn followed Jackie's playing in Montreal, via the newspapers, and took note of the success he was having there. After a shaky start, he became a budding star, leading the league in hitting, making a believer out of his manager, and attracting an increasing fan following, especially among the French Canadians (who were called in some circles "the white niggers" of the city). He was leading the Royals to a pennant. (This is not to say he didn't suffer bouts of racial abuse on the field, and he had to endure those, which hurt him, but avoid at all cost fights or arguments.) Furthermore, as was learned later, his best friends were a helpful Jewish couple, Belle and Sam Maltin. Sam was a Socialist and sports reporter for the *Montreal Herald*, and a stringer for the *Pittsburg Courier*. Belle, who was pregnant, taught Jackie's wife, Rachel, Jewish cooking, and when she found out about Rachel's interest in classical music, took her to outdoor concerts on Mount Royal. (She also knitted a sweater for Rachel, which she wore for many years.) Moreover, they introduced Jackie to their good friend Herb Trawick, a black football player who played for the Montreal Alouettes; and soon Herb became a good friend of theirs too. And they rented, with hospitality from the owner, in a solid white middle-class neighborhood, in the French East End. So Montreal was good, and the right place to launch his career, as Mr. Rickey had hoped. Outside Olympic Stadium today you can discover a handsome statue erected in honor of Jackie, created by a French-Canadian sculptor. Jackie is still remembered very fondly by loyal Quebecois fans.

The great Russian short story writer Isaac Babel once wrote,

"Passion rules the universe," and Jackie, on the base paths, ruled the game with passion, a strange word to employ in baseball nomenclature. But that was his style: he was passionate, provocative, and relentless. Unlike what most fans believe and the media hoist up, an exciting runner will offer more sustained drama and fine passion for a connoisseur than most other players (or parts) of the game, including the home run hitter, simply because of the time spent out there, on the bases. It was the one area where a player could show off his creative flair in a major way. (A fielder like Mays could do so defensively, but the actual time of a great catch is measured in seconds.) Jackie provided that special drama and more. In fact it may be said, or interpreted, that he took out his full pent-up revenge on the base paths, acting as a kind of modern-day native Michael Kohlhaas (the Kleist novella) on the baseball field. It wasn't that Jackie was simply a base stealer, not at all. It was something else, something unique: while on the bases, taking his outrageous leads from first, second, and especially third, he dominated the action, taking it away from the pitcher and catcher, who usually control the action. He became the center of attention, like a quarterback on the gridiron, or a star diva in an opera, and here, the star outlaw of the drama. The highly conservative ways of baseball, decades-old hallowed traditions, suddenly were being interrupted, intruded upon, and transformed.

For when Jackie got on the bases, he became a terrorizing threat, unlike every other player; he performed unusual feats. Oh, there were great base stealers before and after, but no one did what he did on the base paths. He had a kinesthetic awareness of his body—probably an ingrained trait that was honed by his broad jumping, a sport composed of speed, strength, and agility, and his other sports—and this gave him a super refined sense of what he could do on a particular field. For example, to go from first to third on ordinary grounders to the second baseman just didn't happen; but for Jackie, this unspoken rule of the game didn't apply. Or others. He'd tease a pitcher with his lead off of first, or off second; and force him to focus on him, the runner, not the batter. Most irksome, he'd flaunt his provocation by taking a long lead off of third base, maybe ten to fifteen feet (to start with), and, arms dangling, up on the balls of his feet, staring at the pitcher with mockery in his eyes, threaten to run all the way home as the pitcher began his windup to throw. That moment was suspended in time, with Jackie controlling the action and the fans hushed and anticipating, like an extended moment in a great drama. Often he'd charge down the base path halfway, some forty-five feet, stop short suddenly, and then head back to third, *daring* the catcher to try to toss him out. (Each catcher would try, but never catch Jackie, whose reflexes were too quick; but periodically he would throw it wild to third, allowing Jackie to trot home. So, for the most part, they quit trying, and quit looking bad, and allowed the pitcher to take the blame.) So, his third base lead was disdainfully tantalizing, his provocation insulting to the pitcher. In short, his saboteur shenanigans, even when he didn't steal, wreaked havoc with ninety-five percent of the opposing pitchers, driving them to harmful distraction from the batter, when Jackie was on third.

And often he charged all the way home, panicking the pitcher and distressing the catcher, and much more often than not making it safely. As any fan knows, the hardest theft in baseball is the steal of home, since the runner is heading straight in the direction of the pitched ball, and hence avoiding the need for a second throw from the catcher to a base; therefore the odds are far greater of a runner being thrown out than of second or third being stolen. Most base runners never attempt a steal of home in any season or in *an entire career*, and even the very swift ones will only attempt it once or twice in a career, let alone a single season. In Jackie's second year, he stole home seven times, and was caught but once. (One way to measure this accomplishment is to compare it to Babe Ruth's hitting fifty-nine home runs in 1921, while the next batter closest to him, Bob Meusel, hit twenty-four. That vast gap between the first and second hitter of home runs was the surest measure of how great a home run hitter the Babe was. Likewise, the gap between Jackie and every other runner in the stealing of home— no one stole home when Jackie stole seven times—is probably the best evidence of Robinson's unique skill and superiority.) This performance was due to the fact that Jackie put incredible pressure on the pitcher and the catcher every time he made it to third base, creating an attention-disorder dilemma for the pitcher who was trying to focus on the batter, and also for the catcher, who was constantly worried about Jackie streaking all the way home. Such psychological pressure is not to be seen in the statistics; nor is it in any real way quantifiable; yet it plays a significant role in the momentum—and score—of the game, and demonstrates, especially to fans at the park, who dominates the action at crucial moments. And where exhilaration lies.

Let me give another example, by means of a modern comparison. In a crucial last game of the season in 2011 in Baltimore, with the playoffs looming, the Red Sox had a runner on first and third in the eighth inning, with its star speedster, Jacoby Ellsbury, at third base. The Sox were winning 3–2, but desperately needed an insurance run, since their late inning pitchers were having a tough time closing out games. The playoffs were looming if they won the game. The batter, Ortiz, hit a feeble grounder, maybe 10–12 feet in front of the plate, and the Oriole catcher raced out and scooped it, and, checking Ellsbury, who remained standing still, ten feet off of third, the catcher threw down to second to force the runner from first. Ellsbury quietly returned to the bag; the next hitter made out, and no run was scored. The Oriole team tied the game and won it in the ninth, and the Red Sox were out of the playoffs. Now here's how Robinson would have played it, and altered the Red Sox season. Once he saw the Baltimore catcher grab the dribbled ball, Jackie would have been dancing ten to fifteen feet, daring the catcher to throw; the catcher, hesitating for a split second, would then have to decide: throw to third to try to get Jackie? No chance. Throw to second and get the force out on the runner from first and risk Jackie coming home? No way. Take the easiest way out, throw to first, and forget the high-risk plays? But in this case, with Ellsbury playing it safe—and he was a faster runner than Jackie!—the catcher threw to second to get the runner out there, and Ellsbury retreated quietly to third. But for Jackie, that hesitation, that doubt, was all he would have needed. Once he saw the ball leave the hand of the Oriole catcher, he'd be off for home, knowing the ball would have to travel 120 feet to the second baseman and then back 120 feet to home plate, with Jackie only needing 75 feet to get to home; the probability was very high that he'd make it. (I never saw or heard of Jackie being thrown out on such a maneuver.) And the crucial insurance run would have been scored. That's the difference between a mere speedster who could become easily irrelevant, and a mischievous base runner who could cause untold damage. Something you would not see show up in the statistics. And the difference was in getting the extra insurance run to edge the Red Sox into the playoffs.

Hearing Red Barber describe Jack's antics on the bases was a thing of beauty in itself. When Mr. Barber, sitting in a Montague Street studio reading a ticker tape from St. Louis, narrated a daring run or steal by Jackie, I listened to it closely, lying in my bed with my self-created score sheet in my hardbound composition book and a pencil. His southern drawl describing an action of skill and passion afforded a parallel pleasure. His was a narration of radio magic, as Mr. Barber *imagined* how Jackie darted this way, feinted that way, charged and halted, and came on again strong, racing home, all by means of the ticker tape clicking and his memory of how Jackie did it at Ebbets Field, and from his own imagination of how he was doing it out there in Sportsman Park. A feat of Red Barber alchemy, connecting intimately to a boy listening in his Brownsville bedroom. (And connecting to how many other transfixed young fans via a wooden Philco radio?) Such were the passions of childhood, baseball, and Mr. Barber, a radio poet re-creating Jackie at play.

How was Jackie able to steal home so often, and run the bases with such daring success and derring-do originality? (The only other runner in baseball history who supposedly ran the bases with comparative aggression and who instilled such fear, was the legend from an older era—four decades earlier—Ty Cobb. But Cobb's intimidation came in great part from his intentions to maul an infielder.) Naturally, part of the answer was mental, part physical. First, Jackie accomplished the stealing of home by his acute sense of who the pitcher was, what he was throwing (fastball, curve, change), and how poised or panicked he would become when watching Jackie dart, feint, and bluff! He was not, for example, going to steal home off pitchers like Warren Spahn or Robin Roberts, two old pros who were crisp in their delivery, perfect in their techniques, and shrewd in their pick-off throws. Second, his knowledge of the catcher (and the batter, his own teammate) was continually developing and improving, and he always took in the whole situation (inning, score, importance). Third, he was a terrific slider, an underrated baseball skill; his hook slides, for example, wherein he slid around the catcher's tag and caught the plate with his far leg and spikes or with his bare hand, were subtle acts of baseball beauty. It is a shame of those days that we didn't have instant replay or YouTube, for it would have been highly instructive to witness those steals and slides up close and in slow motion, like seeing a ballerina perform a pirouette in perfect detail. (There was the famous shot of Jackie stealing home in the World Series against the Yankees in 1955, sliding just underneath Yogi Berra's tag, and sending Yogi into a tantrum out of embarrassment and anger. Was he really safe, as the umpire ruled, or out, as Yogi always claimed? Let's have the slow mo so we can determine the truth.)

And finally, fourth, his extra edge: Jackie was stealing to make a point—not merely to be competitive—to state his case, to say screw you to the white players who had cursed him and taunted him and punished him for his race, who had kept organized baseball an exclusive For Whites Only club for a hundred-plus years. Stealing home, and doing it rather consistently, and showing the white boys that he was better than they were at their own cherished game and privileged pastime, doing something that not even the best of them (Cobb included) could or would dare to do—this excellence, this superiority was what Jackie had been showing since he was a little boy: being just a little bit smarter and a lot better than everyone else on the playground, school yard, gymnasium, or sporting field. Excellence, achieved by determination, skill, smarts, and chutzpah—that was the Robinson mission, for baseball and for the nation's white audience to witness.

Interestingly, it was only in baseball, where time was slow, and not measured by an external clock, where Jackie could have enacted such theatrical dramatic revenge. Nowhere in the other major team sports—like basketball, football, hockey, all controlled by a clock—was there the possibility for a player to slow down game time, as there was in baseball, for a runner to take his time on the bases, get the pitcher to throw over or check him out, and put the game on a kind of pause control, so he could show off his full array of fierce and fine exploits. In sports like basketball, football, and hockey there was constant contact and movement: running, jumping, or hitting constantly; players were perpetual motion machines, in nonstop games of video proportions and sensations. But only baseball presented a still, pastoral beauty, like some New England landscape painting. Still, calm, green, quietly lyrical. A pitcher pitched, a catcher caught, a batter tried to hit the ball, while the other seven players stood around, waiting patiently, trying to stay focused. For the unknowing, like most foreigners who followed soccer or basketball or hockey, our game was so boring, so uneventful; while for afficionados, this baseball was a thing of beauty. It allowed you to watch, to contemplate, to analyze—something like reading a poem. And yet Jackie changed those terms, once he landed at first base. And it was only in running the base paths, not in hitting or fielding, that a stage was set for his special performance. The subtle rules of the conservative game were always there, officially on the record, waiting for an original performer to take advantage of them, stretch and bend them to his will and talent, and put on a new and exquisite exhibition. Like Nijinsky or Nureyev entering the ballet world, and suddenly performing airborne leaps and magical pirouettes on stage within traditional ballet, and transforming them and redefining the art.

Do I think that Jackie was consciously playing and saying, No, in Thunder! (à la Melville) or explicitly thinking, Fuck You, to the white players and system? Not fully. I am, rather, arguing that there were two drives operating in Jackie, from the contextual evidence of his life. One was to be his own man, a dark-skinned

Negro, proud, assertive, and powerfully independent; and the other was to be a highly intelligent citizen, forgiving and understanding of the context and history of racism, and surprisingly sympathetic to the plight of the whites. In his internal split between sympathies, as it were, I read the playing out in Jackie of the influences of two famous black men and their opposing philosophies, Booker T. Washington and William E. B. Du Bois. The first was the powerful educator and integrationist who never gave up trying to bring Negroes into the mainstream of American life; and the latter was the brilliant writer and philosopher who did give up on the idea of the black man integrating; he moved himself to Africa to be among his own race. To my mind, Jackie embodied that historical paradox—which was to be played out later in a different way and on a different scale by Malcolm X and Martin Luther King—without ever resorting to naming those illustrious Negro predecessors. While Jackie was closer, in his strong belief in integration, to Booker T., and, later, King, he re-embodied—and rechanneled through sports, especially baseball—the anger of Du Bois. When you read his autobiographies, you can sense here and there the turbulence lurking beneath the lines and read his ambivalence in the text. You realize then how much he was holding in, and holding together, inside.

You could never tell it from his face, which he wore as a stoical mask. No matter what the insult or injury, especially in those first years, he would not reveal emotions in his face. Neither in pain, nor in victory. You could not get in. The triumph of a great play, a steal of home, would produce no grin, no hint of a smile. That mask would not be violated, broken through. It was somber, still, dark, unflinching, fierce. It faced you, and said, "Do what you will, judge as you will, you will not break me, or deter me. I am coming at you, full force. I will accomplish my work *according to my will, not yours.*" Jackie's will was to pursue its own ends, its own freedom. That's how I read that mask, especially in the first years of his ordeal.

And yet, torn by the above conflicts and contradictions, he was also his own man, very much so. He was learning as he was going, it seemed, learning how his sporting ability was translating into and nurturing a fuller identity. He had learned this when he found himself recruited by UCLA, again when he joined the Army and became an officer, again when he joined the Kansas City Monarchs in the Negro Leagues, and finally when Mr. Rickey advanced him up to the Brooklyn Dodgers. The son of a sharecropper, grandson of a slave, was moving upward, by means of his athletic ability and determined character. In his bones, you might say, he felt more and more what his native country was about, for good and for bad. The sporting fields had taught him much about his nation and its attitudes towards the Negro, and he absorbed it internally as he grew in outward accomplishment. If he still did not fully grasp or believe the power he was accumulating—or let alone what he might do with that power—that was to come later, as he rounded third, you might say, in retirement, on his way home.

America was gradually taking notice of two things: Jackie was making it in major league baseball; and even beyond, the colored boy was doing things out there that the white boys weren't, or couldn't. He was playing a special style of baseball, developing a new brand of daring, while helping the Dodgers win games. And more and more he was winning over his teammates with his determination and decorum; he was becoming a team leader. (Even the reluctant and skeptical and bigoted, like Eddie Stanky, Bobby Bragan, and Carl Furillo, were being won over.) Something

he failed, we failed. Every steal he made could have been a bone-head play: 'Stupid Nigger!' He was not a dumb man, doing what came naturally. He knew what he was trying to do. And this man, in a very personal sense, became a permanent part of my spirit and the spirit of a generation of black kids like me because of the way he faced his ordeal." Perhaps Roger Wilkens' key remark is, "If he failed, we failed." That remark acknowledges Jackie's iconic burden and identifies him as a symbol of accomplishment.

Jackie was the first black man to cross over into mainstream America, in a *performance* mode, where the stage was a major white field, and the result was a huge splash. This was exciting and important news, a sports story that transcended sports; but maybe even more important, one that went far in boosting the energy, psychology, and core identity of a whole people. Who had done that before except great political or spiritual leaders? No wonder Count Basie and others were writing music and lyrics about Jackie; for the Other America was now in for a long and upward journey. The American Negro was now getting a sense of what it might be like to ride as a first-class passenger, and the new engineer was a baseball player.

Jackie's high level of performance was all the more intense because it was played out on fields of hostility—vulgar, vicious, and open hostility—both on and off the field. Threats, curses, intimidations, physical acts, death-threat letters, the majority of the white world saying no to this radical trial of baseball and democracy. They tested him constantly, and brutally, early and late. Players tried to spike him as he crossed first base, and did so (it didn't help that Jackie was playing first base for the first time in his career, and had to learn how to plant his foot deftly on the base when taking a throw); pitchers threw at his unprotected head—no protective helmets then—and he ducked or hit the ground, got back up, and restrained himself; several catchers enjoyed saying up close the vilest obscenities when he was at bat, referring to his "nigger whore mother," the "coon pussy" of his wife, his "jungle-and-monkey" heritage, and he would have to stand silently at bat, hearing and not hearing, and trying to maintain his focus on the pitcher; some fans and players tossed out black cats onto the field, and some deposited cartons of Aunt Jemima Pancakes by the Dodgers' dugout. Openly bigoted managers, like Ben Chapman of the Phillies, stood outside his dugout and threw out vile racist epithets. Anything to unnerve Jack, cut into his focus, urge him to quit. After work, there were the hotels and restaurants, especially in cities like St. Louis and Cincinnati, that would not allow the team to stay or dine on their grounds because of Robinson and his "stained skin." (While some teammates complained, most were on Jackie's, and Mr. Rickey's, side.) Letters poured in regularly to him and to the team, threatening violence. The psychological pressure was as great as the physical intimidation. Playing baseball, and playing it skillfully and well, amidst the torrents of vulgarity, threats, and open intimidation— all this formed a major challenge, and one that Jack had to endure, live through, and conquer.

I remember a game, for example, when the high-flying Cardinal team came in to play the Bums, in June or July, a lovely summer afternoon. The Cards were a leading pennant contender, and had some of the greatest players in the game: Red Schoendienst, Marty Marion, Stan "the Man" Musial, Enos "Country" Slaughter, Terry Moore. The Cards and the Dodgers were the teams to beat. In about the sixth inning Jackie got on base with a bunt, and then, on a hit and run grounder to second, a simple bouncing ball to Schoendienst, Jack turned at second, and, surprisingly, kept on running. Crazy. But the first baseman's throw to third was a bit late and a bit high, and he made it; and I saw Schoendienst pick up a handful of dirt and fling it away in angry frustration. First to third off the great second baseman *was not done, ever.* Burt and I looked at each other, and shook our heads in disbelief.

In the next inning, however, he was paid back; the Cards were mounting a rally, two men on, and Slaughter, their hustling outfielder, hit a hard grounder to second, which Stanky fielded cleanly and threw to the Dodgers' Reese at second, to start the double play. The return throw to first from Reese beat Slaughter easily, but suddenly we saw Jackie on the ground, writhing in pain. Slaughter looked down, and, grinning with open disdain, uttered a few choice words and trotted off the field. A few Dodgers came over, as Jackie on the ground was removing his shoe, and you could see the blood seeping through his sock. Slaughter had crossed first making sure to step on Jackie's foot with his spikes, sending him reeling. My admiration for the "hustling" Cardinal player went down a few notches. "That's the way it's going to be played for the whole season, I bet," Burt said to me. And I understood. As Rickey had forewarned in his interview. Jackie would be a mark, a target, for his brand of play as well as for his color, and he was not going to be able to retaliate, not that year. And just then, at nine years old, I would lose my idolizing innocence about some of the best players in the league, and somewhere in myself understood that great players could be terrible men.

The overall hostility and atmosphere of adversity took its toll privately, though Jackie stayed cool and collected publicly. Sports writers like Wendell Smith (*Pittsburg Courier*) and Lester Rodney (*Daily Worker*) suggested it, and Jackie himself acknowledged it, in his first (and most moving) autobiography, *Jackie Robinson: My Own Story* (1948). That first year especially was a year of private uncertainty, periods of depression and constant suppressed rage; and real self-doubt and frequent insomnia. (His wife, Rachel, was, along with Mr. Rickey, a steady calming presence.) Though suffering in private when home in his small apartment in the black Bedford-Stuyvesant section of Brooklyn, he continued to display, as the athlete on the field, his superb cool and stoical poise, never giving a hint of his inward turmoil. The pain beneath the poise was never viewed or displayed. (Which made the recent film *42* so wrong, so cartoonish.) And under that severe stress, a pressure cooker of baseball and race, Jackie, as the single dark-skinned player in the white major leagues, never cracked, never wavered. A masked human fortress of mental fortitude. Jackie's steady, cool performance of three-season endurance was not unlike what another black man would have to endure some sixty years later, during his year-long political trial for the highest office in America.

And yet, most interestingly, consider Jackie's reaction in the autobiography—written immediately after the season, and published in 1948—to the waves of resentment and anger. His reaction is an astonishing mix of calm reasoning and understanding, *and even forgiveness, for what white society had put him through.* The hounded victim was showing full mercy toward the racists and predators. For example, when he quotes letters that he received during the season, he chooses those from three or four white fans who are *rooting for him,* and not those from the thousands of haters and bigots. The same goes for ballplayers. He compliments people like Hugh Casey for his support later in the season, but omits mentioning that Casey was among the five or six original Dodgers who protested against having Jackie on the team. And in another instance, after Ewell "The Whip" Blackwell, the Reds' tall and dangerous sidearm pitcher—six foot five inches and pitching off a mound nearly a foot high—lost his no-hitter to Eddie

Stanky, the batter before Jackie, he took it out on Jackie by "launching a blast of profanity and name-calling," then fired the ball at his head. (From behind the plate in Ebbets Field I saw Blackwell pitch, and when he whipped the fastball, the hitter had a split second to pick it up and get down, or he'd be beaned, with no head protection.) But Jackie writes this carefully reasoned and Obama-like justification: "Naturally, such incidents as I have related hurt and anger me, but I think I understand why they occur. In the excitement and heat of a hard-fought game, every nerve in a player's body is keyed to the breaking point. Then something snaps inside, and a good-natured guy suddenly goes berserk for a few seconds. Old, long-buried prejudices and racial epithets subconsciously leap to the surface. I believe most of us are sorry and ashamed after such outbursts, and I'm certain they will happen less and less frequently in America—both in the ball park and outside."

What is truly remarkable here is the measured tone and forbearance of Jackie, coming after the hate-filled first season of abuse and torment. (The autobiography was "as told to" Wendell Smith, the Negro newspaperman who was also his road companion, courtesy of Rickey.) Is this not rather Lincolnesque in its understanding of the American audience and its white psyche? And Branch Rickey-ish in its shrewdness of strategy? Here Robinson was already showing, just after his rookie season, signs of unusual poise and reflection as a citizen, and a mature understanding of what the full stakes were.

For the last thing the country would have wanted or tolerated in 1947 was an angry or vengeful Negro—anything resembling a slave or post-slave mentality—a fellow who couldn't control or handle his emotions while trying to play the game of the white boys. In other words, you couldn't be the angry Bigger Thomas of

Richard Wright's *Native Son* (1940), or the vengeful Nat Turner of slave narratives, or the traitorous "Commie" Paul Robeson, or the feeble Stepin Fetchit, or the comic Rochester of *The Jack Benny Program*. None of those characters would have passed muster, or come through. A different sort of Negro was called for, permitted, or imagined. You had to play the game well, very well, even better than the typically good (and great) white players, and in the meantime take whatever abuse was dished out to you without resorting to the perfectly normal responses of open anger and actual retaliation. If you accepted those supra-demanding terms, and abided by them constantly throughout the spring, summer, and autumn, the nation would take you seriously, and *allow you* to become a certified member of the sacred fraternity of major league baseball players. Handle the pressure, play at a high level, keep your cool, and you *might pass through*.

(A parallel from the world of academics: when Lionel Trilling was the first Jew to be granted tenure in the English department of Columbia University in the early 1940s, a well-meaning department colleague came to his front door, congratulated him, and then offered, "But remember, no more of your kind!" Was a similar thought running in the heads of major league bosses?)

Not only did he "get through" in the playing field, but, subsequently, when he was to reflect upon it in his autobiography, he got through it there too, with a superior grade; his small book is a model of reason, poise, purpose, and restrained passion. *My Own Story* is a quiet tour de force and a brilliant piece of diplomatic strategy, showing a full appreciation of the opportunity presented to him to reflect upon his exacting, tumultuous year. Not surprisingly, the project had been strongly encouraged by Mr. Rickey, who wrote the strategically low-key introduction.

Now the irony here was that Jackie the man—unlike the

player and the writer—was an intense fellow with a quick sense of injustice and a fiery temper (about race), which he had exhibited early on in his youth (Pasadena skirmishes) and again in the Army, and in baseball (with the Kansas City Monarchs). In the Army especially, when he was admonished and called a nigger by a southern officer, Jackie supposedly stood up in his face and challenged him verbally, stopping just short of hitting him. But the main confirmed time, in 1943 in Fort Hood, Texas, he was told to get up and step to the back of the bus for sitting alongside a white woman; actually she was a light-skinned black woman whom he had known; and when the bus driver insisted, and began to bully and intimidate him, calling him nigger, Jackie railed back at him, but didn't budge and told the driver to get on with his driving, and he sat right there. After the bus arrived at the base, officers were told and he was officially admonished. For his insubordination and disturbance there was a trial, and Lieutenant Robinson was brought up for court-martial; but, after a four-hour hearing in which two Army lawyers, both white, defended him, and several of his white battalion superiors defended his character, he was exonerated on all charges by the military court. Jack had held his own, stood up for his principles; but he understood clearly the power of Jim Crow in the armed forces. Soon thereafter, however, for various reasons, including a right ankle injury, he was discharged and received an honorable discharge. (He had spent some eighteen months in the Army, from 1942 to 1944, and perhaps the best part of it was his budding friendship with the young Joe Louis, begun at Fort Riley, Kansas.) Playing for the Kansas City Monarchs in the segregated Negro League, he was rumored to have threatened a bigoted umpire with a raised bat, though this act remains unverified. Branch Rickey knew about these and other incidents (as he had done his homework, using scouts *and* detectives), so he was aware of the dark—the justifiably dark and justifiably defiant—side of Jackie.

More significantly, *BR actually wanted that Baldwin-ian fire in his player*; at the same time he wanted—and required—that fire to stay within, coolly contained. (Jackie would have served as a most interesting model in Baldwin's famous *The Fire Next Time*.) It would be risky for Rickey to bet that Jackie the player, and the man, would hold up his end, and hold on to the volcanic and the cool; but Rickey, the Brooklyn impresario, the judicious gambler, was willing to make that bet. Strains of volatile DNA running through Jackie's blood were part of the package, and desired. There would be Mr. Rickey and Rachel, Jackie's calm and steady wife, to help keep the fire contained, when Jackie's temperature rose for whatever reason: fury or fear or anxiety. Of course on the field he was on his own, his solitary own, for the main trial and testing of that first year.

Emerson wrote, in 1841, at the end of "Self-Reliance": "Nothing can bring you peace but yourself. Nothing can bring you peace but the triumph of principles." There you have one of the basic credos behind Jackie's ability to cope with it all.

Nothing was more testing and pressure filled, on the field, than coming through when needed in the clutch. Whether it was with your bat, or your glove, or your leg or arm, you had to do your job, in the clutch, to prove yourself. For way too many media observers and fans, baseball remains a game of statistics, and too many Hall of Fame members are chosen based on numbers or statistics. Too often this is an easy camouflage, a bogus way of judging. For those who know the game from the inside—the smartest managers and players, and the real fans who watch the game closely—it is the clutch players who are the most valuable, not the statistic makers. Whether it was DiMaggio or Mays playing center field in a necessary game, or Whitey Ford pitching to Ted Williams in the late innings, Koufax or Gibson pitching a crucial game, Brooks Robinson or Billy Cox fielding a sharp grounder at third with the potential tying run on base, you wanted those players there, in the crucial moment. They were not perfect, they made errors, but not when it counted; their percentage of coming through when you needed them most was very high. Into that group of serious clutch players, Robinson merited a secure place. When you had to have the job done, and a little special play beyond one's expectation, Jackie was your man, your player in the clutch. In innumerable games, he often got the important hit, laid down the perfect bunt, stole an alarming extra base, and ran a pitcher and catcher into bad errors of judgment and execution. Ask Campanella, ask Reese, ask Burt Shotton, ask the other managers. Also, ask the knowledgeable fans, like the youthful me, who observed him daily.

For Jackie, winning games was the most important thing, not his individual ego play. And therefore the artful skill of bunting, a seemingly incidental and rather unceremonious task for the big stars, was for Robinson another way of winning. In his second year he had forty-four successful bunts, including fourteen for base hits. This was and is unheard of. Most players never have a base hit on a bunt in their career, and too few know how to do it well enough for a reliable sacrifice. The bunt is to baseball what the sonnet is to poetry, a formal art of compact beauty. The batter has to shorten up on the bat, one hand held low at the handle and the other midway up the shaft, and learn to balance the weight so that when contact is made with the ball, the batter can control the direction of it, toward first or third. And the batter has to get his bat on top of the ball, a ball that may be traveling at ninety miles per hour, so that he can set it down onto the ground, and not pop it up into the air, where it will do little good. In short, bunting is a delicate skill, and most hitters never take the time to learn it. (Especially now in the American League, where the pitcher doesn't bat because of the designated hitter rule.) But Jackie flourished with bunting, using it for thirty sacrifices—moving a runner over one base or bringing in a runner from third—in one season and fourteen singles; he was a master of that lost art.

Once I witnessed him in a most unusual circumstance—one that defines his genius and defies the rules—bunt home a run to win the game. Two outs, last of the ninth, and a runner on third for the Dodgers, and the Chicago Cubs infield playing deep for Jackie, who, at bat, had had an ordinary day, and a hard time hitting the baseball cleanly. With two outs and a runner on third, there is no way you should—or can—be thinking of bunting for a hit; no one did that, because the runner coming in from third can be thrown out easily if the bunt is not perfect. But Jackie had three things going for him: he had enormous chutzpah and confidence in his skill; he knew the pitcher and the infielders (it was now August); and he believed in the power of surprise. Sure enough, the right pitch arrived, and a curve from the right-handed pitcher allowed him to push the bunt to the right of the pitcher and beyond him, towards the second baseman, who, playing deep, had to charge in a long way to try to make the play—either at home, where there was no chance, or to first, where Jackie was hustling swiftly. The second baseman and the pitcher came close to colliding; finally the infielder grabbed the ball and tossed it to first—but too late to get the anticipatory Jackie, who beat it by a half step. The Dodgers, who were as stunned as the Cubs, ran out onto the field to celebrate with Jackie, who was walking back slowly, pigeon-toed, sober faced, as though he had just failed instead of succeeding brilliantly, his cunning play winning the game and informing the fans and players about why he was, already in his second season, the smartest player in the game.

(Contrast this with Ted Williams, the Red Sox star who refused to bunt when the infield played its right field shift for him, leaving only one player on the left side of the infield; how many more games might the Red Sox have won if Williams had thought of the team first, and his narcissism second?)

Perhaps the most famous of Jackie's many clutch plays came in the final series of the season with the Philadelphia Phillies in 1951. In that crucial game to determine the pennant winner, with two out in the twelfth inning and the sun fading and the bases loaded for the home team Phillies, the Philadelphia batter (Waitkus) hit a low line drive up the middle, a sure hit to win the game *and* the pennant for Philadelphia. While a line drive heading to the outfield gives an outfielder a few extra seconds to judge the trajectory of the ball, and to race to get it, a line drive heading through the infield cuts down that time for the infielder by half, at best. In Shibe Park that September day the ball was hit on a low clothesline up the middle, apparently finishing the season for the Bums. Except that Robinson, who had positioned himself towards the middle of the field (realizing a fastball would be pitched), took two quick steps and dived behind second base, and, flat-out horizontal to the ground, snared the ball with full extension. The crowd was stunned and silent. (I was listening to Red describe it live, voicing quiet amazement in his dry southern drawl.) Pee Wee ran over to him, lifting and congratulating him, and three other Dodgers came over to help him as he lay on the ground. And then they escorted him to the dugout. For the moment, Jackie had extended the game, and the season. It was the fielding play of the year, considering what was at stake.

But maybe more—maybe it was the play that defined who

Jackie was, and it symbolized how his teammates and fans had come to trust him to do the possible *and the impossible*. Here is the venerated sports writer Red Smith's description: "The ball is a blur passing second base, difficult to follow in the half light, impossible to catch. Jackie Robinson catches it. He flings himself headlong at right angles to the flight of the ball, for an instant his body is suspended in midair, then somehow the outstretched glove intercepts the ball inches off the ground." The fall, as Red Barber (and his biographer) noted, jammed his left elbow so hard into his solar plexus that he was knocked out. Smith continued, about how Jack was "stretched at full length in the insubstantial twilight, the unconquerable doing the impossible." "Go shake a cottonwood," Barber enthused, from the park. "I don't think I ever saw anything quite like that, and I could barely see it." The *New York Times* reporter Roscoe McGowen wrote that Jack's catch "was one of the greatest, if not the greatest, clutch plays that I have seen in almost a lifetime of watching major league games." I remember the play, keeping score at home, and thinking he was like a real Superman, performing his special feats on a baseball field and not in a comic book. It was even more extraordinary because of the urgency of the moment.

Yet, more was to come that day. The game went to the thirteenth and then the fourteenth inning. Consider what was at stake: the whole season of 154 games, six months of steady work, the pennant and possible World Series. With the shadows falling across the field after six o'clock on the late September afternoon, the last day of the regular season, Jackie came to bat in the fourteenth. Facing the Philly ace right-hander, Robin Roberts, and still hurting from his twelfth-inning crash to the ground, Jackie connected on a fastball and hit a line drive that kept soaring above the field and into the left field stands for a home run. The fairy tale day for Jackie, and for us fans, was complete. John R. Tunis couldn't have scripted it better. Jackie's feats won the game and forced the famous playoff game against the Giants. It was the kind of everything-is-at-stake game, and clutch performance, that defines a player, a career, a moment in baseball history.

Later, in the evening, we kids buzzed about it at our usual hangout, by the blue mailbox corner of Sutter and Ralph Avenues, steps away from the Sutter Theatre. (Like kids on how many other corners, schoolyards, luncheonettes, around town, around America?) The next day at Winthrop Junior High, it was the only talk that counted, spiraling everywhere; even my respected, serious French teacher, Miss Cheyfetz, mentioned it, making her suddenly come alive to our class. (The talk of Jackie's play went on until Bobby Thomson hit his notorious home run a few days later.) It was the kind of performance that, far from being a mere statistic, stays in the heads of the players, the radio and newspaper journalists, the hearts of the fans and kids. Jackie became our Joe DiMaggio. Certainly if anyone had any doubts about his entering the Hall of Fame immediately upon eligibility, that September 30, 1951, day influenced it, clinched it.

Peers too appreciated the higher value of Jackie. Here is the great catcher Roy Campanella, veteran of the Negro and major leagues, viewing him, years later: "Jack was one of the only cleanup hitters who wasn't a home run hitter. He was a line drive hitter. He could bunt a man in from third, and it was impossible to throw him out, but the runner on third with two outs had to be alert to score. He could get the base hit when you needed it. He could steal a base when you needed it. He could make the fielding play when you needed it. Jackie would beat you every way there was to beat you. I have never had a teammate who could do all the things that Jackie Robinson could do. I could extend it even further—I have never seen a player that could do all the things that Jackie Robinson did. Except that he didn't get the opportunity at a really young age. He could've been twice as good. He could think so much faster than anybody I ever played with or against. . . . He was two steps and one thought ahead of everyone else."

That last thought, taking note of Jackie's ability to think and to think ahead, like a Grandmaster in chess, is a most acute assessment coming at the end of Campy's reminiscence of Jackie, and coming from a peer who was a much more conservative personality. A player's sports IQ is different in each sport, but in baseball, especially, the level of intelligence is most observable because of the slowness of the game. It's almost as if the game moves in slow motion, allowing intelligence to manifest itself most clearly; also because the individual player is so easily viewed (as opposed to basketball or football players, where the player is always in a blur of speed, moving, tackling, leaping). The slow pace of the game allowed Jackie to show off his great baseball intelligence in a variety of ways: his anticipation when on base, his knowledge of the particular situation, his understanding of the opposition, his skills at winning in many different and subtle ways.

Indeed this sense of thinking ahead and anticipating was never more manifest than when, in the second year, he switched to second base and teamed with shortstop Pee Wee Reese to form a double play combination, which became the best in the majors. Jackie's anticipation at second, and the timing with Pee Wee, was perfect; those are the necessary ingredients for the most beautiful play in the field. It is the perfect music of the defense, since it involves two or three players, quick accurate tosses, and precise timing. Shortstop to second baseman or second baseman to short, on the little toss or flip of the ball, and then the infielder receiving the ball at second has to avoid the runner coming into second full force, and fire the ball to first to retire the batter for the second out. When it is done right, with the right rhythm and teamwork, it is a pitcher's salvation. When Jackie was the fielder at second, turning the double play, you had the added intensity of watching the runner head straight for Jackie's legs, instead of the base, and Jackie having to leap over or completely sidestep the assault. He learned to do it well enough that by the middle of the second season and definitely by the third, he and Pee Wee were a well-oiled machine, knowing each other's moves and throws, working by instinct and anticipation, and becoming the best in the game, breaking double play records. For the pitcher and the defense, that's *the* necessary clutch play.

So Robinson, the colored boy, the Negro interloper, the grandson of Georgia slaves and son of sharecroppers, was not only superior and exciting, the most exciting player in the game, but he became the man in the clutch when you needed him. Grace under pressure, as Hemingway put it, never suited a player so well. Grace, with style. And he went beyond expectations, or hopes. He never panicked, made excuses, or sought to avoid any of the tests, on and off the field. He was there, with the goods, consistently. Consistency, with style. This counted, in baseball as in war, for a great deal, especially while the huge local and national audience was watching—and privately, wittingly or unwittingly, grading his performance. Once again, things were going on in the collective unconscious of the nation—like perceptions, attitudes, instincts, judgments—that myths, personal and national, are made of.

Let's go back a bit. If Jackie was to be tested for the (white) major leagues and, on another level, for the Republic, Rickey had to provide a safety net for his ebony tightrope walker, a harbor of safety and sympathy for Jackie. It started with Mr. Rickey himself and Ebbets Field, then Red Barber and the right manager (Burt Shotton) and player (Pee Wee Reese), and a cordial Negro sportswriter, Wendell Smith (*Pittsburg Courier*), who would also be Jackie's roommate on occasional road trips. Plus of course the fans of Brooklyn, who were growing in numbers and in passionate enthusiasm. As the novelty wore off and the unique excellence of Jackie became apparent, Brooklyn and Ebbets Field became a distinctive site, a kind of Shakespearean island where magical things were happening: spirits and bodies and strange storms all swirling around. And presiding over the curious island was a wise magician who wore a bow tie and Benjamin Franklin spectacles and smoked a cigar, an unlikely Prospero, Branch Rickey. In other words, amidst all the waves of anger, scorn, resentment, uncertainty, fear, fury, incredulity, disbelief, Mr. Rickey was giving Jackie a solid platform to perform on, and a launching ground for transformations. After all, Mr. Rickey was seeking to transform an ingrained tradition, a set of tacitly understood values, a nation's way of thinking. In its social and moral importance, the Brooklyn Project was matching the Manhattan Project, and was in some ways more important to the body politic. For here in Brooklyn something unusual was happening; magic was being performed. The real and the poetic (or mythic) were intertwined.

The country had been transformed before, by politicians, generals, presidents, philosophers, historians, maybe novelists or movie directors, but never by a baseball player. Ruth had captivated a nation by means of his home run power and outrageous behavior and personality. "Shoeless Joe" Jackson and the Black Sox Scandal had commanded the country's attention. Then there were the marvels of baseball lore: DiMaggio hitting safely in fifty-six straight games, Lou Gehrig playing in over two thousand games consecutively, Cy Young winning over five hundred (511) pitched games, Ted Williams seeing the stitches twirling on a curve ball as it arrived at the plate, and so on. But Jackie the baseball player hit something deeper—infiltrating the nation's consciousness, and subconscious, as well as pricking its conscience. Newspapers, national magazines, radio outlets, ticker tape communications followed his progress and through a media microscope. It was not merely a sport that Jackie was excelling in and affecting; he was affecting a country—what a country believed about itself, by means of a sporting Negro and through him its whole history, and its future, concerning race. Almost accidentally, via the parallel world of baseball, America was beginning to face itself in ways that were peculiar and unexpected, and that Gunner Myrdal had hoped for but was not seeing in his 1941 classic. The challenge was freshly put and natively arranged.

Indeed, before Jackie, Negroes for the most part had been shadow souls in white society, flitting in and out as servants, porters, pimps, shoeshine boys, movie extras, radio foils, minstrels, barely visible folk in white America (it was only in 1952 that Ralph Ellison was going to posit and publish his *Invisible Man*). They also existed as fine and serious entertainers of one sort or another—the likes of Louis Armstrong and Billie Holiday and Duke Ellington in jazz, Jesse Owens and Joe Louis and Sugar Ray Robinson in sports, Paul Robeson and Marian Anderson in singing, Richard Wright and Langston Hughes in literature, Booker T. Washington and William Du Bois in folklore—but none of these figures was acknowledged as a substantial American citizen, influencing the essential body of the society. (There were also the dangerous Negroes, like the runaway slave Nat Turner and the great boxer Jack Johnson, who would steal and plunder and violate white women, and burn white houses down in endless riots. They were the black ghosts haunting our white national psyche.) Those floating translucent figures existed in their own segregated territory of colored folk, a kind of murky ghostly world, but in white mainstream society they were mere shadow figures—half real, half ghosts. Part of this selective myopic vision was due to whites' own history of slavery, and inherited white guilt from that history, and part from the closed gates of the contemporary white world. Whites saw only what was around them, not beneath or beyond. It was Jackie, and Jackie alone, who, by crossing over into major league organized baseball, turned his ebony shadow self into a convincing and *real native* self—not a slave or post-slave self—one who reconstituted his Negroid blackness into an acceptable native hue. *He might have been ebony in color, but he was becoming American in substance.* This was a remarkable transformation coming from one individual, and not an entire movement, in the body politic of a whole society. After all, who had done such a thing before in our history? Washington, Jefferson, Lincoln, FDR? Only our greatest national heroes. But a baseball player, and a Negro to boot? Now that would have been a million to one shot in Vegas if they had laid odds.

As Jackie proceeded through that summer, it was becoming clear, beautifully clear, that he was driving the Bums to a surprising result: the National League pennant. Yes, the Dodgers had several other players of contributing significance, such as Bruce Edwards, Pee Wee Reese, but it was Jackie who was the engine driving the machine. Even Dixie Walker, the southerner and Brooklyn "Perple's Choice" favorite, confessed this: "No other player with the possible exception of Bruce Edwards has done more to put the Dodgers up in the race than Robinson has. He is everything Branch Rickey said he was when he came up from Montreal."

Coming from Walker, a major signer of the spring petition to refuse to play with a Negro, this meant everything about how much Jackie had earned, on the field and off, the trust and admiration of his teammates (as Bobby Bragan, the once-bigoted catcher acknowledged, "Jackie made me a better man").

To be sure, Jack's stats for the year were not immediately striking; they were, let's say, interesting. He batted 297, hit twelve home runs, knocked in forty-eight runs. The nearly .300 BA (batting average) is the only impressive number here, since few rookies hit for that high a percentage. But when we move further into the numbers, we discover that he scored a huge 125 runs, second best in the National League and by far the best on the Dodgers. His twenty-nine stolen bases and twenty-eight sacrifice bunts (!) were also tops in the league. (Catchers then were far more accomplished in defense.) Further, he bunted fourteen times for base hits, an unusual record. (If a batter nowadays gets more than a few, he is considered an artist.) Only four times did he fail to get on base or advance a runner when he bunted. This fact attests to his remarkable use of the bunt as a weapon, and his exquisite skill with bat control. And his willingess to find a way to get on base, and to win. Furthermore, he led the Dodgers in games played (151), at bats (590), hits (175), total bases (252), doubles (31, tied with Walker), and homers (tied with Reese at 12). Jackie was the locomotive, the engineer, the true guiding spirit.

And we felt the force of that spirit striking like an electrical current, all through the borough, via the radio and the newspapers and subway word of mouth. Brooklyn rode along with him, following in his path of high passion. Before the pennant was won, in mid-September, the Dodgers and Brooklyn acknowledged his special achievement and created a Jackie Robinson Day. A genuine first, this event, which never happened, before or since, with a rookie player, for any team in the history of the league. Why would a city celebrate a player so early on, even before the team had officially accomplished anything? Because Brooklyn recognized what he had been going through—his baseball and racial trials—and had already survived and succeeded. Branch Rickey (and Bill Veeck), had been right: *Brooklyn was the right site, the perfect place,* to try out the Jackie experiment. (Jackie had attracted into Ebbets Field the largest number of fans in the ballclub's history, and far more than any other National League team had, attracting 1,807,000 in a bandbox that held approximately 34,000. How many would he have attracted if the seating held as many as Yankee Stadium, approximately double that size?)

So that when he came onto the grassy field, accompanied by his entire family, on September 23, 1947, he became, semiofficially, Brooklyn's baseball hero on the first steps of his journey towards iconic status. At that singular event, Jackie received a host of tributes: the dancer Bojangles Robinson saluted Jack as "Ty Cobb in Technicolor"; the borough president, John Cashmore, and a fan, Jack Semel, gave him an "interracial plaque"; and he also received a variety of gifts, such as fine cutlery and silverware, a console television set, and, most notably, a new light gray Cadillac. (Not too bad, this last gift, when Cadillacs still counted.) Wonderfully, his mother Mallie made her first airplane trip in from California. A woman who had started out in Georgia sharecropping, she took the bold risk of transporting herself and her small boys on a train to a territory unknown. With a full house in attendance, and thousands more listening via the voice of Red Barber and, later, RKO newsreel, Brooklyn displayed its full appreciation and poured forth its huge love. Jackie was now a part of the city's folklore, like Walt Whitman or Coney Island, the Gershwins or Henry Miller. Imagine, the birth of a genuine folk hero in his first year.

And three days later, a motorcade took the team from Ebbets Field to a holy reception at Borough Hall for the celebration of the pennant. A major event. What may be described as a blind date back in the early spring grew into an engagement as the summer wore on; now Jackie's betrothal to Brooklyn had become a true marriage. For better and for worse, no matter what, he/we would be joined at the hip. (No wonder Jackie wouldn't leave Brooklyn when the team moved to LA.) Fittingly, on that day, the *Sporting News* gave Jackie the Rookie of the Year Award, an ironic award, given that the famous sports weekly had, earlier in the season, derided Robinson as a talent, and denounced the idea of integrating baseball. So much for expertise. Furthermore, on September 22, *Time* magazine put Jackie on its front cover, seconding Brooklyn's appreciation and giving a high passing grade to Mr. Rickey's test. The passion for Jackie generated by Brooklyn was now spreading around the country, and the marriage of the pair was recognized and nationally consecrated. We in Brooklyn were intertwined with him. He was ours, and we were his, in a separate State of the Union space, you might say. That's how big baseball—and *Time*— were in the late 1940s, dominating the sports and sharing the national scene.

My father took notice of all this, which was strange for him, a Russian Jewish immigrant who took very little interest in American sports of any sort, his only interest being soccer, a foreign sport. My father appeared to the world as a European gentleman, dressing in formal suits and neckties, for example, when he went down to his club in the evenings—a storefront Brownsville club used for pinochle and chess that had served as an air raid wardens' center during the war—making sure to shave at 6 p.m. for the second time of the day. A Bolshevik Communist (and a Zionist), as well as a social snob and a domestic bully, Harry (or Herschel) believed more in Stalin and Lenin than he did in DiMaggio or Dixie Walker. He came to enjoy prize fighting, once he discovered that a good middleweight, Harold Green, lived across the street from us on Ralph Avenue. And, after dressing us both formally, me in my knickers suit, we would walk up to Eastern Parkway Arena to see the Friday night boxing matches. (Some pretty good pros, too, including the likes of Gus D'Amato and Floyd Patterson.) Furthermore, whenever any European soccer team came from abroad to play in Brooklyn, like Manchester United or the Jewish Hapoel, he'd drag me to one of those ridiculous games, since it was a silly sport, having no native stars or familiar players that meant anything to me. And imagine going up to Bedford Avenue to see a British or Jewish team playing soccer, in *my Ebbets Field*! A sport of kicking a ball without the use of hands? But baseball? Harry couldn't fathom it, calling it a *goyishe narishkeit* (a gentile foolishness). Nor did he want to fathom it. A native boorishness, not worth his interest. Until Jackie came along.

Then, rather astonishingly, he grew interested. He began hearing all the buzz from the outside, so to speak, from the daily newspapers that he read, the *New York Post* and the *New York Times*, and even the left-wing *PM*. Not to mention the *Daily Worker*, which he occasionally read, where the excellent reporter Lester Rodney had been following Robinson and his progress from the start. And also from the inside, our family; he paid attention to my travels to Ebbets Field with Burt (Bream), whom he knew was taking me to the games and was not happy about it. He and Burt had always had an adversarial relationship, politically and personally, Burt being like an older brother to me, and also an outspoken opponent of my father's Communist beliefs. So, curiously enough, Robinson slipped into being a sort of shadow member of the family, a paradoxical figure to be employed, and exploited, in different ways.

As the disaffected son, I began to use Jackie as a wedge, a way of separating myself from my father, both personally and ideologically. As my father became more interested in baseball through Jackie—because of his breaking through the color barrier and exposing our country's bigotry—and wanted to learn all about the rules of the game, I dismissed his entreaties casually, paying him back for his violent harshness towards me and my mother. Further, I used Jackie as my own idol, my American hero up against father's Russian political icons. Of course Jackie was far greater, since this was baseball, and not politics, about which I couldn't care less at the time. And in that guise, Jackie became my benefactor—unbeknownst to him—in the sense that he helped provide me my authentic American identity, against the Russian identity that my father wanted to pin onto me. And the fact that I had actually met Robinson twice, and had been favored with his written signature and gravelly voice and words of support, made him that much more of a personal benefactor and hero. So he would mold and nurture me in such private ways, which neither he or nor I could have imagined.

The irony was acute: here was my foreign father, seeking to understand baseball and Jackie, for political reasons, while his nine-year-old son was using or manipulating baseball and Jackie, against that father, for personal reasons. A perfect symmetry, you might say. (Plus, there existed the further irony, more asymmetrical, of Jackie seeking a more complete American identity, out there in the big white world, while I was using him to build up and create my own, within my own family, and beyond.) Such were the strange ways of Brooklyn, 1947, and left-wing politics, a boy and his father, and the many roles of Jackie Robinson, visible in public and invisible in my family. A baseball god, a personal hero.

Of course there were other kids like myself, Jewish kids, who also came to see Jackie as their hero. The thirty or so kids from my immediate neighborhoods—from Brownsville: Kassover, Kamph, Steve Werter, Norman Dennis, Ronald Tavel; and from East Flatbush: Schlossy, Heshy, Lloyd Brown, Richie Boodman, Jackie Greenfield, Maxwell Mendes. They were in awe and semi-disbelief when they saw my autographs from Jackie. They wanted to know every word and every gesture of our small meetings. But all over Brooklyn—and the country—kids were starting to bond with Jackie, because of his rousing brand of play and his underdog status, making him their baseball idol. He was becoming a genuine Brooklyn folk hero—to the kids, where heroes resided and icons were created. The Midwest had Paul Bunyan; the South had Daniel Boone and Davy Crockett; New England had Johnny Appleseed; Native Americans had Crazy Horse and Geronimo; and now Brooklyn had Jackie Robinson. We were making progress, catching up, getting even. Gradually, over the next few years, the newfound hero of Brooklyn was taking on full status as a kind of folk hero across the land.

As I said, all the Jewish kids were lining up. Take my friend Martin Sherwin, who lived over in the heart of Flatbush, and who, later on, won a Pulitzer Prize (for a biography of J. Robert Oppenheimer). Here are Marty's words about the influence of Jackie when he was a boy in Brooklyn: "Jackie Robinson was the Barack Obama of my youth. My parents were apolitical, conventional Democrats. They loved Roosevelt but their credo was to keep their mouths shut and heads low. Nevertheless, they passed on to me some way a true hatred of racism and a sympathy for the underdog. I think it ran more or less like this: We are Jews and we have

been discriminated against unfairly. It is our responsibility therefore to stand up against those who discriminate against others. We
were all Brooklyn Dodgers fans and Branch Rickey did this unbe-
lievable thing. He hired a Negro, and this Negro was handsome,
smart, well spoken, calm, and in every way attractive. And there
were people who hated him because he was a Negro. Unbeliev-
able. It was just like what the Nazis had done to the Jews. Jackie
was therefore one of us. And he was my hero. I switched from
shortstop to second base, changed my number to 42 [we were a
softball team named The Arrows and we had jerseys]. I followed
every slight he received and his triumphs were in some weird way
Jewish triumphs to me."

For icing on the cake, Marty added, he even tried to walk
pigeon-toed, as Jackie did, but it slowed him down instead of
speeding him up, so he gave it up.

The Jackie fever was spreading all over the borough (and
beyond), infecting most kids, like Marty, myself, and how many
countless others? Newspapers gave the headlines, but not the street
talk and schoolyard passion. There were hundreds of thousands,
easily, from our borough alone, for whom Jackie had become an
overnight hero. Marty's Jewish observations are particularly sug-
gestive, since they refer also to the community of adult Jews and
Jewish immigrants, not merely their sons, *who felt with Jackie*, for
some of the very reasons mentioned above. (Remember, one-third
of the borough was Jewish by 1950.) Take the case of Dr. Ray-
mond Raskin, a prominent New York psychiatrist who, at eighty-
eight, remembers performing his medical residency at Beth Israel
Hospital in lower Manhattan, where he and the other mostly
young Jewish doctors were caring for a number of European refu-
gees from the Nazi concentration camps. Once Jackie joined the
Dodgers, Jackie became a focus of radio attention and adoration,

via Red Barber; and so, while those young doctors cared for the wounded Holocaust survivors, Dr. Raskin and colleagues, even those who were not particularly baseball fans, listened to the Dodgers games and rooted for Jackie. Another fine irony of Brooklyn history is that the exciting Negro rookie was gathering a cult following in all sorts of curious corners, including that special refugee ward of the kosher Beth Israel Hospital, at East Seventeenth and First Ave.

Another curious corner. I remember going on a late summer errand for my haberdasher father over to Red Hook, a tough section where Irish and Italian steamfitters and metalworkers worked at the Brooklyn Navy Yard. They were first- and second-generation immigrants, with different accents and new—for me at age ten or so—curses and obscenities. After delivering some embroidered ladies' hats for my father, I stopped at a neighborhood luncheonette for a quick sandwich and soda. The place at lunchtime was full of men with yellow hard hats, a few Navy men, and some locals; while I put my order in at the counter, I noticed the side wall. Set on it were two framed photographs, one of a new Navy cruiser ship recently built right there at the Yard, and the second a group photo of the Dodgers baseball team, with scribbled signatures across the photograph. Over the cruiser ship was the fall launching date, and set over the baseball photo was a handwritten banner, saying, "Welcome Aboard, Jackie!" I was taking a good long stare at it, trying to make out the myriad signatures of Furillo, Reese, Jorgensen, Hodges, Branca, Erskine, Snider, and Jackie. Presently, a broad fellow with an apron put his arm around me and said, "Are you a fan, kid? Purty, ain't it? Well this is the year for our Bums, with Jackie MVP!" The white working-class enclave, known for its tough guys and raw prejudice, had come aboard.

Of course in the Negro neighborhoods like Bedford-Stuyvesant, the excitement grew to fever pitch. I remember walking up there, along Rockaway Avenue in the late 1940s, and seeing all sorts of Hail Jackie signs, hats, buttons, T-shirts, decals, and framed *Time* covers in the windows. It was as though the black Messiah had arrived, and had settled down in Brooklyn; and this was many years before Rosa Parks, Malcolm X, or Martin Luther King Jr. I made sure to wear my own Robinson Dodgers T-shirt and hat, and felt the pride emanating through nods and smiles. What had previously been an off-limits district for walking about had become a turf of pride and welcome. Even up at rowdy Boys High Jackie made things easier, gave Negro teens hope—a fact confirmed again, later on in my Jefferson High, when I had a close friend from Bed-Sty.

In sum, Jackie was becoming a symbolic figure for the whole underrepresented (and immigrant) population; he symbolized the classless, minority underdog who was breaking through the fixed status quo, and gradually, though perhaps not just yet, entering into the mainstream. He was in the midst of demonstrating that the power of merit—even in, or especially in, white baseball—was more important after all in the national fabric than the powers of prejudice and bigotry; and therefore, that our underlying ideals of meritocracy and fairness were alive and getting better in 1947. His baseball excellence and growing popularity was providing the best compelling evidence. Again, Jackie was doing it in behalf of everyone on the bottom, it seemed to many, everyone who was striving or looking upward. By means of his Thoreau-esque individualism, and resistance as a player and man, Jackie was proving to be a kind of transcendental force—an Emersonian Idea—not merely a skilled baseball player. But with this new twist: this force was stained ebony, like one of the slaves of Emerson's era of the 1850s come back anew, nearly one hundred years later, as a baseball player, a most unforseen redeeming force of the modern era.

Was there another country where such dramatizing of a moral idea, such social and existential transformation, could have been acted out by a sports figure?

Clearly, as I've suggested, inside my family he was becoming a force too. As my father struggled to learn more about this peculiarly native game, and thereby get closer to me, Jackie became the crucial figure in our unusual chess game. He was a knight or bishop on my side, making sure I was to be an American, not a Russian, boy, and opening up my sadly exiled father—who had always wanted to return to his beloved Russia and his family there—to the ways of this strange land of democracy. There in my Brownsville tenement at 701 Ralph Avenue, Jackie became my secret weapon, energizing me in my family conflict, and creating a way forward, practically and emotionally.

What a fine paradox: Jackie, the outsider in society, became an insider in our apartment, a personal tutor educating the father and benefiting the son. Interesting also, how he remained a benefactor for me later on when I was to write my first short stories in my early twenties (early 1960s) about home ground and a father-son conflict, in which Jackie figured prominently. And some twenty-five years after that, when I wrote an autobiographical novel, *Brooklyn Boy*, Jackie (and Brooklyn) again played a significant role. For example, in a section of some thirty pages devoted exclusively to the Dodgers, I wrote a section on Robinson, called "The Stranger." And in there I went over the nature of the strangeness, the fear and anger it invoked, and the hostile acts that Jackie endured, including some choice epithets that the catcher would invoke as he stood at bat, reminding him of his slave heritage, and his gorilla family, and of the smell of his wife's "nigger pussy," along with "Black Sambo" name-calling from the visitors' dugout, and the tossing out of the black cats onto the field. In recalling those painfully evocative moments from my youthful days at Ebbets Field, I also returned to my two exhilarating post-game meetings with the sober, ebony-faced man, and his forceful words to me while laying his hand on my nine-year-old shoulders. Words and a presence that lingered on through years and lay like a long benediction upon my soul.

So in the 1990s he remained my spiritual guide, not an Italian Beatrice or a Jewish Maimonides, but a native baseball player, at my side while I pursued the writing career that I had told him about in real life, in the parking lot outside Ebbets Field. What an unlikely Magwitch to a Brooklyn Pip.

And in the meanwhile Harry (or Hershel), the Russian father, was learning a paramount lesson about America and democracy, via Jackie and his on-the-field exploits and off-the-field progress. Here, on home ground, things changed, and not always according to Marxist or capitalist doctrine; in fact, changed mostly in strange and unpredictable ways. Russia may have been his Motherland dream, but America was his son's reality.

While putting pressure on opponents, Jackie was putting pressure on the country as well. Could a single individual put pressure on a country? Think about it. Maybe a political or moral leader with a momentous decision to make, a Lincoln, could—to preserve the Union? An FDR—to join the war? A Truman—to drop the bomb? A Martin Luther King—to March in Selma? Certainly, not ever, a mere ballplayer. Yet as I've said, because of the era, the circumstances, and the history, Jackie was becoming more than a player; he was edging into myth, a living and playing myth. Was he not in President Harry Truman's mind, for example, when he integrated the armed forces in 1948, a year after Jackie's breakthrough? Or in Martin Luther King's youthful mind, as he surveyed America's race situation and formed his own activist way forward? As King later noted, "Without the shoulders of Jackie Robinson, I wouldn't be here today." Jackie Robinson was evolving into "Jackie Robinson, a symbol of native fair play, an American do-it-all." He was becoming, and embodying, an Ideal, based on our highest principles and declared values.

Each sport has moments and situations in which a player can put pressure on an opponent, and force an opponent to play beyond his means or skills to cope with the pressure. A player on defense in basketball, like guards Walt Frazier or Dennis Johnson, can operate as a defensive force by means of their long hands, sense of anticipation, game knowledge; they become a disruptive force. In football, you can have a defensive line (as with the 1985 Bears) or a special linebacker, like Lawrence Taylor of the Giants, disrupt an entire offense. In baseball this feat is much more difficult to accomplish, since the defense is simply fielding the ball, in reaction to a batted ball. By definition, while the defense here is passive, once the ball is hit to them, it controls the action. But Jackie changed the terms there, as I have suggested, by finding a way to pressure the opposing team *without hitting the ball*—by running the bases with his brilliant instincts and daring skills. ("Poets are like baseball pitchers," Robert Frost once wrote. "Both have their moments. The intervals are the tough things.") But Robinson, though not a pitcher, turned the tough intervals into sequences of aesthetic beauty and vitality. That was his gift and, you might add, his baseball charm. And he did it by thinking faster, anticipating a few steps ahead, as Campanella said. Who could have imagined that the slope-shouldered, pigeon-toed awkward fellow who lumbered from home and looked in pain when he walked, would become a Fred Astaire on the bases, dancing, feinting, gesturing, glittering? (An Astaire with vengeful pleasures and boyish skills.)

Baseball first, the nation next, this seemed to be the logic of the evolving process. Gradually, and increasingly, through his diamond prowess, Robinson was moving beyond the borders of the game and *putting pressure on the country*—to assess and take stock of itself, and maybe, just maybe, start to transform itself. Jackie represented "the American challenge" that Professor Myrdal had posed in 1941, and, six years after the book, was demonstrating sudden and surprising progress. Catching the country by the ear, as it were, and spinning it around to look at itself in the mirror. Dealing with race by means of a small, hard, white horsehide ball and a Louisville Slugger ash bat, a leather glove and spikes, in a totally native game. And at the same time actually embodying some basic principles of the American Idea, as posited by our Founding Fathers and, later, by Emerson and by Lincoln.

Moreover, Jackie kept coming on, kept getting better, kept honing his adventurous style and seeing his influence spread and grow more prodigious. Both on the national agenda, and in the schoolyards, gymnasiums, and parks, where his name was on everyone's lips, between plays or while hanging out. In places like Betsy Head Park in Brooklyn, a rough and Negro-tough place to play basketball with bent steel rims: "Didja see that steal of home? Shee-it!" or "Man, can you believe he got outta that rundown and scored?" In the gentler PS 189 schoolyard and in Lincoln Terrace Park, on the softball fields: "That cat makes more special plays in one or two games than the rest of the league makes in a season! Holy Moly!" And in the Prospect Park's Parade Grounds baseball diamond: "See what Jackie did yesterday to the Cardinal pitcher? Mungo got so frustrated by that bunt he spit out his tobacco and threw his glove on the ground!" Or, while getting a lime rickey or an egg cream at the Sutter Avenue corner luncheonette, a friend suddenly shifted into base runner mode to show me how Jackie took his lead: "Ya see, the arms are dangling, for leverage, and he's on the balls of his feet, and he keeps going out a mite farther, a mite farther"—blocking the way of a New Lots IRT passenger— "daring and almost grinning at the pitcher . . ." Yes, right there on the asphalt street (or dirt) of our native turf, where we kids hung out or played sports day and night, Jackie was The Man, the top dog, giving our Bums the extra juice, making them as exciting and powerful for us as a new Broadway play by Arthur Miller or Tennessee Williams, or a musical by Rodgers and Hammerstein, was for the adults. Except that the adults, too, of all sorts, were following Robinson's exploits with increasing interest. He was not merely a subject for the sports fans, but also for the intelligentsia, the hoi polloi, the police and the lawyers, the *Times*, the *Tribune*, the *Daily News*, the *Post*, even the *PM*, the borough president and his bureaucrats, the new and old immigrants. On the field, he was as splashy as they come, creating his own style of excitement and urgency every time he hit, fielded, or ran.

It didn't hurt that Jackie, off the field, led a quiet and ordinary middle-class life, wearing no fancy jewelry (see Jack Johnson), flashing no pink Cadillac (see Sugar Ray Robinson), hitting no clubs, bars, or strip joints. Rather, he was a strong family man. At home with his clear-eyed wife, Rachel, and their newborn son, Jackie Jr., he lived quietly—no scandals, no skeletons in the closet—further reassuring everyone in the borough and beyond that Jackie was wild and adventurous *only* on the bases or between the foul lines. Otherwise he was a regular citizen, like ninety-nine percent of Americans. Furthermore, he not only dressed well, in a conservative manner—suits, ties, raincoat—as did his gracious wife, but his residences increased his image as a solid citizen on the rise up the mobility ladder—from a tiny apartment in black Bedford-Stuyvesant to a classier place in the East Flatbush neighborhood of Brooklyn, then to a residence in Rego Park, Queens (near Ella Fitzgerald and Count Basie), and finally, several years later, to an expensive suburban home in Stamford, Connecticut. (When I was attending Winthrop Junior High School 232 in East Flatbush, we sometimes took a small detour and walked past the Robinson brick townhouse on Tilden Ave., hoping for a glimpse of our new baseball God. Once a few of us saw him, and we waved and he waved back, and though it was like seeing Clark Kent, not Superman, it was the talk of the evening.) He was climbing—and choosing to climb—all the right steps upward on the ladder of success, further ensuring his respectability and credibility to a wide white audience. Jackie may have been a very dark Negro, but internally, he was clearly one of us in values and beliefs—so went the native signaling. Black was now mingling with white. How productive for his future, and how wisely Mr. Rickey had scouted, chosen.

Already in his first year Jackie was crucial in helping the Dodgers win the pennant, as he led the league in stolen bases, with twenty-six, led the Dodgers in games played and runs scored, and paved the way for them to play in the World Series. (Why was the league led by Jackie with only twenty-six bases stolen, when in later years, the numbers went much higher? Catchers in those days were chosen more for their defense and their throwing arms, and their ability to handle a pitching staff; and since there were many fewer teams and fewer catchers, the quality was much higher; and pitchers were trained much more precisely for holding runners closer at first.) The *Sporting News* gave him the Rookie of the Year Award. This meant that he was as important to the team as the two other leading Dodgers, Bruce Edwards and

Pee Wee Reese. Apart from peer and league recognition, he was afforded the truest coin of success, national credibility, from the conventional sporting magazines like *Sport* and the *Sporting News* to the *Herald Tribune* and the *New York Times* and *Time Magazine*. And as we have seen, the borough of Brooklyn and its officials and fans formally appreciated him too, giving him his own Jackie Robinson Day at Ebbets Field in September, and presenting him with those gifts on the field, and a ten-minute standing ovation. For any player, but especially for a rookie, this was unprecedented. The dark outlaw was becoming a full-fledged member of the team and of the Brooklyn family, dazzling baseball heads, and filling hearts, in a relatively short time.

Moreover, as Mr. Rickey had hoped, Jackie filled Ebbets Field seats, and seats in other stadiums as well. Number 42 pushed Brooklyn attendance to 1.8 million, the first of ten straight million-plus years of attendance, for all the ten years that Jackie played. (In salary Jackie earned $5,000 for that first year, $12,500 for the next year, and in 1950 hit the jackpot, earning $35,000, the most in Dodgers history.) And he boosted National League attendance to its highest ever number, over ten million. So he quickly had become, as Mr. Rickey had imagined, a major entertainment *and* a commercial hit, not merely a freak in a sideshow as many had predicted. Again, the baseball diamond was the main show in the nation then, a social place to come and to relax with the family, to see others and be seen; and citizens were laying down their money to see the splendid attraction. And not just to see a phenom with a fastball or a prodigy with a violin, but a twenty-seven-year-old rookie of ebony skin and unorthodox style. But what he was doing, and who he was, was enough to draw the fans in, like Ruth and the Yankees did a few decades before. Jackie and his Dodgers were the new hot ticket in town, and you paid to see the skills and feel the electricity. And, truthfully, it was real. Rickey the impresario had done his job, selecting perfectly, choosing the timing—when things were booming and optimistic, and the baseball commissioner was Happy Chandler, an independent soul from Kentucky with an open mind who, despite fifteen owners voting against it, allowed Robinson into the league; and Jackie the actor was doing his part, playing his two parts (player and man) well and with dramatic flair. And when Jackie played in the World Series, in 1947, it was another milestone, as he was the first Negro player ever to do so. Though the Bums lost in seven, Jackie acquitted himself very well, getting seven hits to tie Reese for the most in the seven game series. In front of everyone as they watched, measured, judged.

(And as Yogi Berra, the Yankee catcher noted, and predicted, with Robinson now on the Bums, the Yankees would not go on winning them all. And as usual, Yogi's clarity was right on, as he was a shrewd baseball analyst beneath his famous comic aphorisms. Indeed Jackie took the Dodgers to six World Series in the next ten years—an astonishing feat, truly—winning it all in 1955, Brooklyn's one and only victory in the big one, and against the Yankees. With Jackie as their guiding spirit and most resourceful player, the Dodgers became the dominating team in the National League, for the next nine years, competing with the Yankees.)

Mr. Rickey gave him special, though intentionally modulated, praise after the season. Here are some of Mr. Rickey's careful words from his foreword to *My Own Story*:

> Jackie is well educated, as we generally understand that word.
> He is a good sportsman and a gentleman. On the field he has
> proven himself to be a good player with fine physical skills
> and most unusual aptitudes.

His appearance with the Brooklyn Club in the spring of
1947 was marked in a most singular manner. He had never
been a first baseman; his knowledge of the position derived
exclusively from observation. He did a grand job as the regular
first baseman, and helped materially to win the National
League pennant for the Brooklyn Club.

His greatest achievement, however, in my judgment, was
his tactful handling of his relationship with his fellow players,
as well as his opponents; and the fact that he was able to maintain the favorable regard of the press and the public.

Jackie is naturally a competitor—a combative competitor.
He resents unfairness or unsportsmanlike play directed toward
his team or himself. Under no circumstances, however, could
he allow himself to show resentment. Only those on the team
know the great patience and self-control he exercised continu-
ously throughout the season. For this exemplary conduct, displayed both off and on the field during the entire season, he
deserves the commendation of everyone.

The book bespeaks the modesty and tact characteristic of
his playing and general demeanor. I hope in this new venture
that he will have a sympathetic audience; I hope the sportswriters and fans will receive his book as readily as they have
received his work on the playing field.

Branch Rickey uses certain phrases of interest here, such as
"most unusual aptitudes," and "tactful handling of his relationship with his fellow players" and "a competitor—combative competitor," which he combines with Jackie's "great patience and
self-control." Here is the maestro's shrewdly understated appreciation of the characteristics of Jackie, which helps explain how
Jackie achieved his necessary credibility.

Yet, it is rather interesting to see how, in his last paragraph, Mr. Rickey downplays the true style of Robinson's play—daring and dangerously provocative—by emphasizing the gentler elements of tact and modesty, a more acceptable note for the general reader and fan to come away with. Our wise "Mahatma" (one of Rickey's nicknames) is never short on political strategy or rhetorical prudence. He was the Prospero of the Brooklyn Isle in more ways than one, not only arranging for the right player to come along, but also for the right sort of book to be written by him. The magician behind the scenes, in bow tie and wire-rim spectacles, was using directorial skill to make sure that his favorite phrase, "Luck is the residue of design," was being demonstrated.

Maybe Jackie's baseball and human success had the most important influence when, in his second season, two other Negroes were recruited and brought onboard, without further protest, to the Dodgers. Very soon both of them, Roy Campanella and Don Newcombe, became leading players; Campanella became the outstanding National League catcher for years to come, and Newcombe, a top-notch starting pitcher. Two immediate hits. (Campy's hitting powers and all-around catching ability were enhanced by his easygoing, sunny personality, a striking contrast to Jackie's stern and furious determination. Just as, later on, Campy's simple conservative instinct to avoid any race controversy became a sharp contrast and irritant to Jackie's open civil rights passion.) And over in the American League, the Cleveland Indians brought in Larry Doby to play center field. He was a powerful, fleet-footed fielder who would soon become a staple of the great Cleveland teams. In just a few years, Negro players would be counted among the very best players in the majors, from Campy and Larry Doby and Sam Jethroe (the speedster), to Luke Easter (Indians) and Monte Irvin

(Giants) and later, in the 1950s, to the two all-time greats, Bob Gibson (pitcher, Cardinals) and "The Say Hey Kid" Willie Mays (center fielder, Giants).

(Of course the older colored greats from the Negro Leagues, legends like Josh Gibson, Buck Leonard, youthful Leroy "Satchel" Paige, Willie Wells, never got a chance to display their talents. Although Satchel Paige arrived—in his fifties!—and pitched astonishingly well, considering his age.)

Jackie had led the way, the first dark skinned player to go through the door, and soon the first ambassador easing the way for other Negro players to join the big leagues. What Mr. Rickey had started, Robinson continued and completed in a rather short time. Single-handedly—with his avuncular godfather behind him—he was changing the nature and face (and color) of organized base-ball, a game and status quo that had not changed since its inception nearly a hundred years before. Had he failed—for professional or for personal reasons, for anger or for foolish ways—who knows what the future would have held for integration in baseball? Would there have been any? Or, for the image of the Negro in America?

Over the next several seasons, every major league team—with the Dodgers leading the way—meaning every big city where baseball was played, started adding Negro players to their whites-only roster. (By 1953, for example, seven teams had Negro players, twenty-three in all; and when the Yankees still remained all white, Jackie called them out on it publicly on a radio show, infuriating Yankee fans.) Blackness was becoming visible on the playing field more regularly now, as Negro players were more and more making their mark as players of high quality. Cities like Cincinnati, St. Louis, Chicago, and Philadelphia, bastions of baseball segregation, and urban segregation too, were seeing the influx of Negro ball players, and the soaring rise in Negro attendance, increasing the fan base vastly. (Ironically enough, it was Boston that was the very last team to hire a black player, the same Boston Red Sox that had first worked out Robinson and two others in 1944, a purely token tryout held by the southern owner, Tom Yawkey.) At first these fans came out to see Jackie play; but in ensuing seasons, they came out to see their own team's Negro players play. And most of them, like Doby, Campy, Newcombe, Monte Irvin, Minnie Minoso, and later the great Mays and Gibson, were huge hits, becoming stars or superstars. In other words, once the firm boundary of color in baseball had been crossed, and crossed successfully, what followed next, gradually but inevitably, were citizen and civic boundaries. There were no riots in the streets or stands, and if groups sat with each other only in segregated groupings, so be it. After all, Irish steel fitters from Bushwick, or Navy Yard workers from Red Hook, or immigrant Jewish kids from Brownsville/East Flatbush, or young Italian toughs from East New York, these different groups didn't exactly intermingle; they all clung to their own turf. But what had happened was that now a *whole new Negro presence was seen and felt at these stadiums*, both on the field and in the stands, and the national pastime was becoming truly national in its game attendance for the first time. Simultaneously the significant changes on the field were being extended beyond the stadiums and translated into the consciousness of the whole population. Two men, one a player, the other his general manager/director, had caused this radical shift.

In my Thomas Jefferson High in Brooklyn in the early fifties, for example, I had a small group of Negro friends, mostly from the basketball team, but also a friend from the baseball club. For those fellows, Jackie was not merely a Negro star like Armstrong (Louis) or Fitzgerald (Ella) or Louis (Joe), but a daily living legend, a breakthrough hero, a *visible American* icon, of a different order of honor from those other stars. For Jackie was not only a sensational player, a Dodger who lifted them to their new level of excellence, but he accomplished all that in the "other" world of white players and white fans. He was a crossover superstar. In Jefferson High, which was then about sixty/forty white and black, Jackie raised self-esteem tremendously in the black population. He had won over a borough and was, in a local way, a radical model the way that perhaps Daniel Shay was to the farmers in Massachusetts. Robinson gave teenage Negroes a vibrant hope, set a valiant goal, and dramatized daily a valuable lesson. And unlike the intellectual Du Bois or the civil rights activist King, or the singer/actor/radical Robeson, Robinson was a sports star, something the majority of the kids all played, understood, related to, desired. This was America, after all, where sports was dominant. In short, Jackie was from *their* world, making a difference and *counting* in *the other* middle-class white world.

And even in today's world, if you go to the downtrodden and rough neighborhoods in Los Angeles, like the Crenshaw and Compton areas, Jackie remains the acknowledged symbolic hero, his name on elementary schools and high school fields and stadiums. His name signifies an automatic iconic model for those black street kids. (Plus of course in his hometown of Pasadena, at his John Muir High School and other fields.) And some six decades after his heroics on the baseball diamond of Ebbets Field, he is still The Man to all mature blacks, players or otherwise, the one who opened the doors for others to come through. On the other hand, surprisingly, he is less known to young black kids in other tough urban 'hoods around the country, Detroit and Atlanta, Baltimore and New York, Chicago and Cleveland. There, in the trenches of teenage schoolyards and playing fields and ballparks,

Jackie often exists as a name only, a ghost from the past, much to the displeasure of the likes of Spike Lee and Cornel West.

(And yet, just recently, in the 2014 Little League Championships, a team from Chicago was named Jackie Robinson West; they had won the national championship and played with real spirit on the base paths; I wonder how many of those kids knew about the man behind the name of their team?)

A small summing up: so Jackie had a twofold function in the game—first, as a great and resourceful ballplayer, and second, as the original and successful ambassador, resulting in more Negro players entering the big leagues. And gradually, as Jackie increased his obvious talents in the majors, the player Jackie Robinson grew into the legend of "Jackie Robinson," a symbol of all that was possible in the game—and arguably beyond the game—*if you gave him the opportunity*. Also, just as significantly, Jackie had brought to the sport a kind of athletic—and aesthetic—excitement which was quite different from the usual routine of white baseball, the home run or the double play or the steal of second. You could say that his was not a normative game, but something else, something beyond the norm. He had created a fresh and innovative game between the lines, within the rules, a new way of playing and winning, and a new means of stirring things up in the game, in a sport known for its repetitive and conservative patterns, and too-often boring predictability. Looking at it from this perspective, Jackie had opened up the game of baseball itself, infused and changed it, the way only a few of the true originals from the older era did, such as Ruth and Cobb, Cy Young and Walter Johnson, and a few others. But, unlike those greats, Jackie did it by hurdling a whole other set of obstacles set before him, both on the field and off it. Certainly a Pulitzer Prize for Sports—or a Myrdal Nobel Prize for Peace—was warranted for his accomplishment.

TWO

Jackie's Voice

Overleaf: Ebbets Field, all-star game,
July 12, 1949, Brooklyn, NY
Credit: TSN Archives

If **Jackie's last years with the Dodgers** saw him on the decline as a ballplayer, it also saw him become much more outspoken as a player on the field, and much more so as a civil rights activist. For five or six years he had played top-notch baseball, achieving enormous success—he was even voted the MVP of the League in 1949. There were three reasons for his decline: injuries to his knees, the change in ownership from Branch Rickey to Walter O'Malley (and the forced departure of Rickey), and diabetes. It was the saddest thing for us to see him hobbling about, like a wounded veteran, and to see him openly disgruntled with the new, weak manager, Walter Alston, who never really appreciated Jackie (or later on, Sandy Koufax). Not a smart fellow, Alston, and probably bigoted. And then, when the banker/lawyer O'Malley attempted to trade him to the cross-town Giants, the humiliation was almost complete—until Jackie pulled the plug by refusing to report and play. (And this after Horace Stoneham, the owner of the Giants, offered him a huge paycheck approaching the crazy salary of $100,000 and even a blank check to be filled in by Jackie if he would come over. Jackie declined.) Nor did we fans, or his baseball peers, know how bad his chronic diabetes had become, dragging down his overall health, energy, power, and gradually destroying his eyesight. The last act of the tragedy was unfolding before our eyes, though we—and his teammates, and the media— barely understood the full story.

But there was the other side, the new vocal Jackie. After his first year he began talking, and fighting back, and after his next year or two he opened up even more and let his rage and fury fly out. As the physical side of the player waned, the emotional and political sides waxed. And the voice rose. (Amidst the poisonous air of the Cold War.) It wasn't ever just about him, but also about his people and racial equality. This didn't always sit well with others, including teammates—like Campanella, a much more conservative figure. All this was in the context of what Jackie went through and accepted, and refrained from answering. But when he started to let loose and reveal his fiery inner passion, he was viewed as a different sort of Negro. Consider this from Irving Rudd, the Dodgers publicist and good friend: "Robinson was a man among men, a powerful man, an intellectual . . . who had at first to take being called a nigger by some imbecile. He had to release some of those frustrations later . . . and when he did there were always those who wanted to find fault with him." Indeed many did, when they gradually learned that he was a man, not a saint, and a citizen, not just a ballplayer. The fans came along, even if some, along with some of the players, didn't, or wouldn't. We, his most faithful, the cadres of youth, supported him totally; he was still our hero, still our baseball god.

Yet here is Monte Irvin, the first New York Giant Negro and great player, commenting: "Some of the problems Jackie had, he created for himself. Jackie probably had a little rougher time than anybody else would have had because of the aggressive, abusive nature that he had. If Campanella had been first, he would not have had as rough a time. Campanella is talkative, gregarious, he's likeable. Jackie was not. It got to the point near the end where some of Jackie's teammates didn't even like him." An interesting critique, but it may say more about Irvin's attitudes towards Jackie than about the reality; for it avoids the fact that it was Jackie whom Rickey chose for precisely his characteristics of toughness, intelligence, restrained anger, and heroic stoicism. (Campy remained always amiable and cordial, even after his terrible auto accident, which paralyzed him.) Since Jackie in his first years was not permitted to be either aggressive or abusive, in any way, shape, or form, was Monte missing the truth intentionally?

A colleague of Jack's, Ben Wade, thought differently: "If some didn't like Robinson, it was for no other reason than he was black. He took it for a long time. Right at the end of his career he said, 'I've taken it long enough; now I'm gonna get back and say what I think.' He said some things that I didn't like, but he certainly had the right to say them." And here is the noted journalist Stan Lomax, who viewed him with a more balanced eye altogether: "In his last few years he was paying off people for those indignities that happened to him whether they were there when they happened or not. He got pretty short tempered. I wasn't bothered. I knew the handicap under which he started. . . . He was paying off debts . . . and maybe we should balance things." Jackie was bruising feelings, yes, and while it hurt some, for others it was understandable.

In these last years, the tragic third act began, with new indignities and old virtues re-energized. He became a vigorous and openly combative player, taking no more insults quietly, arguing with umpires, keeping up his reckless-abandon style when he could; but clearly he was running more slowly, playing with injuries and with less speed, less flash. Moreover, he had put on some weight, developed a paunch; his joints were aching, his hair was graying, and he was nicknamed, by some writers, "the old gray fat man." That was a little like calling Captain Ahab "the old gray fat man." But Jackie, like Ahab, kept up his fury, his bile, his earned vengeance. Which made him more controversial, more outspoken, more difficult to take, more fierce in demeanor and words. No wonder Irvin and others had a tough time "liking" or "enjoying" him. He was no longer in the "entertainment" business of baseball. This Jackie was a fatigued veteran of the Great Baseball Race Trial, a wounded soul. And maybe, like Hemingway's veteran soldier in "Soldier's Home," who comes home only to discover that he can no longer fit in let alone bear his old ordinary life, Jackie was not one to reconcile with newfound pleasantries and euphemistic acceptances. His memories of humiliation and racial insult remained all too fresh, while his body—the splendid vehicle for all his lifelong triumphs—now was failing and hurting him.

Fittingly, it was his close family and private friends in Pasadena who had comforted him between seasons, and who truly knew his suffering. (We in Brooklyn knew little of his internal pain.) As his sister, Willy Mae, observed: "When he came over, he used to talk sometimes about the things that had been done or said to him. . . . They took their toll on him. He said that if it had not been for his people, that he was doing it for his people, he would have quit after that first year. It was really too much for any human being to take." A poignant and powerful testimony. As was this, on a related subject, from his childhood friend Sidney Heard: "Jack did a lot of talking about Rickey. He used to tell us how he loved Branch Rickey; he used to tell us how Branch Rickey was the only father he remembered." At home, then, in southern California amidst family and friends, Jackie opened up, spilled his heart and guts; while in Brooklyn, among fans and reporters, he stayed calm, cool, and stoic. A negotiation, which worked, but with its psychological cost. It revealed the chasm between the perceptions of white folk, even the faithful and true-Dodgers-blue, and the underlying reality of what the black folk at home were allowed to see. There, his deep stress, beneath the mask, was openly revealed.

More indignities and injuries followed in his last years, when Walter O'Malley forced Rickey out in 1950, in a business squeeze, and ran the team. A narrow-minded, petty, and deceitful business-man who was jealous of Branch Rickey and his years of friend-ship and glory with Jackie and Brooklyn, O'Malley treated Robinson with annoyance and disdain, as did Walter Alston, the new Dodgers manager who had replaced the likes of Burt Shotton and Charlie Dressen and Leo Durocher, all great fans of Jackie. (O'Malley accused Jackie of feigning injuries, which enraged him.) One time the passive-aggressive Alston and Jackie almost came to blows in the clubhouse, Jackie not backing down from Alston's indifference about a terrible call on the field, but it was broken up by Hodges. The disgrace increased when, first, in October 1956, O'Malley tormented Brooklyn fans by demanding that a new stadium be built and paid for by the borough, then crushed Brooklyn by selling Ebbets Field to a real estate developer; and added further insult in December by trying to trade Jackie to the Giants. Jackie, the personification of the Dodgers in those excit-ing years, declined to go, as I have said; and when the snarky O'Malley made a secret nighttime deal with Los Angeles, Jackie again gave his Bartleby-like "I would prefer not to" response, refusing to go to Los Angeles to join the "new" Dodgers out there. There was only one town for the Dodgers, Jackie claimed, and that was Brooklyn. So he retired and left baseball and went to other worlds, and never looked back. (Once, a few years later, when Stan Musial met Robinson in Manhattan, and asked him if he missed baseball, Jackie said not in the least. How remarkable.)

The whole series of venal episodes shell shocked and wounded us all in Brooklyn, deeply. From the borough president and city officials—like Robert Moses, who was not going to give O'Malley a free ride in the form of a free stadium or land, which Los Ange-les was willing to do—on down to us, the young and old fans and average citizens, the news was astounding. The Great Betrayal had commenced, without Jackie of course. How could they have treated the Dodgers (and Ebbets Field) and Jackie Robinson, our two most sacred icons, like disposable waste? How could the National League allow the team to be moved to Los Angeles, when the Bums were, and had been, *our* team? How could Jackie have been tossed aside? Leave it to Branch Rickey to articulate the right words for the pain and betrayal. "It was a crime against a community of three million people to move the Dodgers," he argued. "Not that the move was unlawful, since people have the right to do as they please with their property. But a baseball club in any city in America is a quasi-public institution, and in Brooklyn the Dodgers were public without the 'quasi.' Not even a succeeding generation could forget or forgive the removal of the Dodgers to California. Oh, my, what a team they were!" How perfectly put.

Indeed Brooklyn never recovered, for when a crucial part of its "body" was removed—its field and its team were its physical shrine and heart—the soul gradually withered. (See the pertinent title of the fine social history by the architect Elliot Willensky, *When Brooklyn Was the World, 1920–1957.*) Where else could the people of the borough gather to worship, if the sacred shrine and its boygods had been shipped into distant exile in the middle of the night? (And look at the Brooklyn of today, a fashionable town known for its high-priced condos, chic cafes and restaurants, gentrified shops and renovated districts—a destination for Manhattan yuppies, for artsy out-of-towners, for well-heeled blossoming bohemians, a town resembling so many others. This Brooklyn has little relation to Jackie's Brooklyn, when it was indeed a unique site in meaning, in feeling, and in the imagination.)

After the middle-of-the-night departure, people went to churches and synagogues and prayed and cried, and heard pulpit speeches imploring the powers that be to set things right again in the borough and the universe. The Borough of Kings was in mourning. (The only thing like it was when Gil Hodges was in his awful battling slump, and the priests and rabbis and citizens said prayers for him.) Curious elegies emerged. For example, at the respected Hebrew Educational Society (HES) in Brownsville, where I used to play basketball and occasionally dropped in on an interesting presentation, I heard a lecture by a Brooklyn College classics professor, who, supposedly talking about Sophocles and Euripides, claimed it would take years before our grief was relieved, and that our situation was akin to a Greek tragedy. And we citizen fans were needed to fill in the place of the bereft, bemoaning chorus. While I didn't understand the exact terms, I understood the meaning. This was a very serious matter. The packed audience asked questions, angrily, and acted as though we had lost a piece of our territory to a foreign country. And then, at the end, Jackie was mentioned, and suddenly, amazingly, he appeared on stage, wearing a sports jacket and white shirt and blue Dodgers cap. He waved and smiled, and the audience rose to its feet in cheering ovation for maybe ten or fifteen minutes. The only thing close to that appreciation for me came years later, in Moscow, when the ballerina Maya Plisetskaya danced in *Swan Lake* at age sixty-one, and afterwards was cheered by her fans for a solid twenty minutes. Our ballerina, however, was male, ebony-colored, and had danced magically on baseball's dirt paths. What a coda at HES.

And to Jackie's everlasting credit, when he was offered even more percs and plums from the Los Angeles he had grown up in, he still declined to join the big move (and betrayal), saying the only Dodgers team that he wanted to play for was right here, in the borough of Brooklyn. (Again, I would suggest he was akin to

Melville's Bartleby, whose five memorable words, "I would prefer not to, " stood for the resistance of his will in the pursuit of its fullest freedom, no matter how high the cost.) So, way beyond the field, he remained to us a man of high principle, not merely a great player, a splendid soul who honored the home turf and his fans; he stayed with us, like a Walt Whitman, a George Gershwin, a Brooklyn icon. Whitman, Gershwin, Robinson—a city could do worse.

Meanwhile, my father too had gone into serious decline after my mother locked the door on him for some abusive behavior towards us, and, after a period of no contact, Harry would wait to meet me once a week to give me my two- or three-dollar allowance. And at each of these grim meetings, in the shadows under the IRT El, by Dave's Blue Room on East Ninety-Eighth Street, he brought up two subjects regularly: his hoped-for return to my mother and the household, and his progress with understanding baseball and following Jackie. After his usual lament and plea to find out whether my mother was ready to take him back, which I rebuffed swiftly, he would turn more optimistically to Jackie. He had begun following him, closely, and even reading the sports pages, he explained, something unheard of in his life. After all, he had been a semi-intellectual, interested in left-wing politics, and American sports were beneath him. An embarrassed smile would come to his face, and he'd acknowledge his mistake in never attending a game with Burt and me. He'd shake his head. "Yes, foolish." But then his face lit up, as though hit with a sudden idea. "But, you know, Sonny Boy, I would really like to see him play. Maybe we should go sometime, just you and me?"

But I was not ready for such late-life compromises and concessions. I said, "No, I don't think so."

He stared at me, first furious, then soft, and shifted directions. "Well I will tell you he's the best gonif (thief) in the game; there is no one like him; he can steal anything! Oy, what a *sheygitz*!" And he began to relate some of the things he had been reading about him, from *Sport* magazine—a far cry from *PM* or the ILGWU union paper—and from Lester Rodney, the *Daily Worker* writer. "He has changed the sport, don't you think?" He laughed lightly. "But it did take me a long time to understand what was meant by, he was 'stealing home.' What an idea!" A pause. "So what do you think, boychik, about all this talk of leaving Brooklyn? They would never let the team do that, would they? Abe wouldn't, would he?" The reference was to Abe Stark, the important citizen who was to become the borough president and whose sign beneath the right field fence, "Hit me. Win a Suit," was famous, a fellow whom my father had gotten to know during his air raid warden years. He smiled weakly. "What a *meshugenah* country, isn't it? A baseball player and a *shwartzer* changing the whole country, and for the better!" I was impressed by his new understanding and how far he had traveled into the game, and how this connection with me now lightened his despair. Having given him enough of my time, I broke things off, leaving him in the moving shadows while the IRT El rumbled overhead. Too bad Burt wasn't around anymore to see the late transformation of the old Bolshevik to a baseball neophyte and Jackie follower.

I remembered my old Dodgers and the old borough with a life-long passion, paying homage to Ebbets Field and to Brooklyn in the same autobiographical novel, *Brooklyn Boy*, where I also honored Jackie. Here is a little of what I wrote about the home field, in 1991, in a section I called "The Shrine."

The square-block, three-tiered coliseum curved to a bow front, with a blue and white striped awning marking the front entrance. In Paris it might have been the entrance to a fashionable brasserie or café; here on home ground it was an entrance to a baseball field. Sacred field. Above, from the roof, flew the two important flags: the Stars and Stripes and the Dodgers banner. The oval building, lined with rows of old-fashioned arching windows set into the reinforced concrete, always seemed to take on a pinkish-golden tint when the sun splashed it. As though nature, along with the natives, saw fit to honor the site. For this building, with its emerald diamond shining within, was the place of true worship, the shrine visited weekly by a hundred thousand or more religious devotees, devout followers since childhood, the long faithful. Opened in 1913 in honor of Charlie Hercules Ebbets (the manager of the Brooklyn Bridegrooms, in 1898), Ebbets Field demanded more devotion, afforded more pleasure, struck more pain, than any church or synagogue in the borough. The Italians had their Popes, the English and French their Kings and Queens, the Russians their Czars and Empresses, and we, our Dodgers. Glories versus glories. . . .

Everyone came to the games. I mean it was a democratic, popular service conducted out there. Baseball was the American sport in those days, the true religion for a free and easygoing people who had their own ideas about independence and good and evil, and their own notions about pomp and ceremony, play and devotion. And with the prices so right, $1.25 for grandstand, $2.50 for lower grandstand, $3.50 for boxes, plus the $.60 for the bleacher seats, well, everyone could afford to show up. The steamfitters and shipbuilders from the Brooklyn Navy Yard wearing their high school windbreakers; the bigwigs from Borough Hall or business execs who worked uptown in Manhattan, loosening their Windsor knots; the "hard-guys" with DA's and pegged pants from Bushwick or Greenpoint, toughs you wouldn't want to meet on their turf; the Negro families from East New York and Bedford-Stuyvesant, dressed up in pressed sport shirts and sports jackets for the memorable occasion of watching the new Negro stars, like Jackie or Newk or Campy; the old-timers with straw hats who remembered the game from near the turn of the century, and kept mental notes of the singular players and moments (from Zack Wheat and Dazzy Vance to "Pistol Pete" Reiser banging his head for the third time against the center field wall); and on weekends, the pairs of fathers and sons from Bensonhurst, Bay Ridge, East Flatbush, Sheepshead Bay, Williamsburg, Canarsie (or transplanted grandfathers and grandsons too, from Westchester or Long Island). All citizens of good and noble faith, of all religions and races, made the pilgrimage to the Shrine maybe once or twice a month, like an instinct or gene or religious devotion pulling you there. Like the Christian pilgrims trekking to Canturbury Cathedral, we the Faithful trekked to Ebbets Field.

And for good reasons: beauty, relaxation, tribal warmth, folk art. Forget the sweatshops, forget the class wars, forget the family troubles, forget the racial antagonisms, forget the daily grind, forget the Depression and World War, forget the anger and quiet despair, forget the ordinary. All the subtle art of baseball, put on display by the Dodgers of those days, would wash away the above, and engage you in elegance and agility on the green diamond.

If Jackie was an unusually gifted player, and an unusual recruiter opening the door for other Negro ballplayers to follow onto the field, it will come perhaps as a surprise that he became a different sort of ambassador outside the lines, especially if we posit the notion that there were several Jackie Robinsons. There was the fierce competitor who would step back from no adversary, and beat him at any game or in any sporting match; and the instinctive fair-play peacemaker, who understood deep down what and where the boundaries of the sport ended and life in society began. He did this as a competitive kid and youth on the Pasadena playgrounds, as a superior college player in three sports at UCLA, as a defiant lieutenant in the Army, and as a rebel player with the Kansas City Monarchs. He would beat you on the field, all fields, but afterwards always treat you like a good citizen, a well-intentioned fellow. (There was the extraordinary case of how, after losing the pennant to the Phillies in 1950, he walked all alone into their clubhouse and congratulated all twenty-five white players and white coaches on their victory over the Dodgers. Picture that scene of gusty sportsmanship, and the amazement of those Philly players.) What an unusual human package and set of oppositions in one man.

If we consider these dual inner roles of competitor/conciliator, and combatant /truce-maker, we find a very complex Robinson, or series of Robinsons: the Jackie who remembered his childhood, youth, and young manhood of fighting bigotry and prejudice, and simultaneously the Jackie who conquered all on the playing fields, and won over his white opponents, and even made many of them admirers; the man who understood, instinctively—and even empathized with—the painful contradictions and living dilemmas of race: the white fear, the disdain, the denial of history and himself, the Dark Other; but also his white peers' hidden or sublimated reservoir of human sympathy, which he needed to stay open to in his heart. We should recall that in practically every stage of his athletic life, Jackie had an older white mentor or protector, someone who believed in him and valued him as a player and man, from several coaches at high school and then at UCLA, to an Army defense lawyer, to a Dodgers scout, to his lifelong friend Branch Rickey. (Plus the legions of loyal white fans he made along the way who followed and rooted for him.)

All those figures helped Jackie pave the way for his sporting career, and probably spoke to him—whispering within—that not all whites were bigots and haters, and that there was hope for racial understanding, personal evidence for reconciliation. (Not to mention the many bigots whom he had converted, like Casey and Furillo, Bobby Bragan and even Dixie Walker, and the hundreds of opposing ballplayers, like the southern manager Clay Hopper of the Montreal Royals, who at first didn't want Jackie to play on his team, and then, once he saw him play and sustain that level during the season, became one of his biggest fans. Or the millions of white fans around the country who were open bigots or secret racists or close-mouthed skeptics.) So, once again, it is worth seeing these poles of opposition working within Jackie: the spirit of integration and hope of Booker T. Washington, versus the will for Negro separation and black power of William E. B. DuBois. At different times in his life, one battled the other and each was a force within him; each created its own tensions and oppositions, and though the one—integration and reconciliation—won out clearly, the opposing force ran fast and hard as an undercurrent.

Was Jackie the man able to hold together his several selves smoothly, integrate them within, or compartmentalize himself seamlessly? Or did he, rather, hold together with rubber bands and band-aids the anxiety and cutting stress, the enormous pressure? From the evidence of his own words in his autobiography, and also of clues from friends and teammates, and from Mr. Rickey, he lived constantly with the pressure of his different performing selves, on and off the field. But he kept it in, behind his mask of stoic discipline. (Though it should be added that playing the game, being on the field, was his true home turf, where he was able to be himself, furious, fighting, and innovative; and yet, paradoxically, relaxed and cool too, because in the game, he was inside his best and surest self.) We remember that he visited the doctor/shrink a few times, up in Montreal, during his days off there, and later on, he visited his "personal shrink," Branch Rickey, when things got too hot. While the nervous breakdown was avoided, the internal stress was not, and the fever stayed high. There is little doubt that the psychological stress, as Rachel Robinson has noted, added to his deepening diabetic illness—which caused near blindness at age fifty, not to mention his arthritis, etc.—and helped cause his premature death at age fifty-three. His was a short but remarkable life, powerfully compressed, filled to the brim with passion, pride, persistence, and pressure.

He was a man of parts, in a uniquely American way.

Those several Jackie Robinsons were on display in the late forties, when he was asked to testify at a House Un-American Activities Committee (HUAC) hearing in 1949 on Paul Robeson, the famous Negro singer, actor, and ex-football star. Robeson had claimed that American Negroes would not be willing to fight on behalf of their country in a war against Communism, and Jackie, encouraged by Mr. Rickey, testified against that antipatriotic position, and on behalf of the strong loyalty of American blacks. Even though at the time he was ambivalent about speaking out against Robeson, whom he admired, he did want to assert his own strong view on Negro patriotism. Later on, he was sorry he had argued in front of the committee. Well, let's say he remained ambivalent, since he very much believed in a principled loyalty to his country. Near the end of his life, he remembered his performance at the HUAC with keen regret, praising Robeson and criticizing his country for its racist positions. (In 1972, a year before his death, in his third autobiography, *I Never Had It Made*, he wrote: "I have grown wiser and closer to the truth about Americans' destructiveness. And, I do have an increased respect for Paul Robeson, who . . . sacrificed himself, his career, and the wealth and comfort he once enjoyed because, I believe, he was sincerely trying to help his people." (What a shift in feeling and perspective for this late Jackie.) The general situation of Negroes in America, which had touched and injured him personally, was set alongside the country that had nurtured his talent and eventually turned him into a fabulous star in his late twenties, and even a mainstream national celebrity—as evidenced by that cover story in *Time*, September 22, 1947. His life was, on one side of the coin, an American Dream come true, and on the other, an American Nightmare of bigotry and racism, from childhood on. This duality held Jackie, defined and pained him, and never released him.

Another Jackie Robinson emerged in the early fifties when, after signing on to work for the popular Chock Full O' Nuts coffee chain as a public relations executive—which he did for seven years, the first Negro to be elevated to such a position by a major company—he then surprised everyone by becoming a special assistant for community affairs for Governor Nelson Rockefeller, the Republican governor of New York, who employed him, in part, to defend his unpopular state policies in Harlem. This especially shocked liberals, but Jackie, the exciting ballplayer and rebellious young man, remained, as a mature citizen, his own man and a convert to capitalism (for his people). He was one of the first Negro celebrities, if not the first, who became a true black capitalist, joining other blacks to participate in Negro businesses and ventures such as the Freedom Bank in Harlem, and the Jackie Robinson Construction Company. It was ironic for the grandson of a Georgia slave and the son of a sharecropper and a cleaning woman in Pasadena to become a Republican spokesman and an entrepreneur capitalist! What a curious evolution, to say the least.

But for most of us old fans, the new politics and political gestures meant little, for we were Jackie devotees, and no matter what he did or said, we were having his back. He had not abandoned us by traitor-ing off to LA, and we were not going to abandon him because of his Republican ties or beliefs. That independent soul was in our hearts, a member of the family. What he had done for us on the baseball diamond was what counted, what we remembered. And what he had done for Brooklyn, giving it a true and unique soul that was the envy of America, was not forgotten.

Perhaps even more disheartening and bewildering for his liberal followers was his temporary support of Richard Nixon in 1960 for president. Yet this needs to be explained. He initially spoke to John Kennedy—after Hubert Humphrey, the candidate he wanted most, lost out—but JFK insulted Jackie by asking him how much money it would take to buy him onto his side. With Nixon, it was a case where his point man promised Jackie that he would work on advances in civil rights for Negroes. When this did not come about, Jackie promptly left the Nixon camp. In short, Jackie was willing to work with any presidential hopeful who was promising a strong civil rights agenda. Once again his people came first, ahead of political parties or candidates or personal gain. Still, certain friends and some old onlookers had to be asking, Was Jackie kidding? What was the deal? Was this the same Jackie Robinson who had fought his way up to the top from the playgrounds, from prejudice and poverty?

Yes, and no.

For *this* Jackie Robinson had been sorely tested and was by now clearly fatigued, his hair now snowy white, his health growing desperate from the diabetes and near blindness, and the high blood pressure working against his heart. Moreover, he had just lost his first son—twice, you might say: first when Jackie Jr. became a teenage heroin addict and, later, after he had recovered in drug rehab, losing his life at age twenty-four in a car accident on the Merritt Parkway, driving home to the upscale family residence in Stamford, Connecticut. (The years of torment thrust upon Jackie from the drug ordeals of Jackie Jr. cannot be overestimated.) In retrospect, then, Jackie's turning to the conservative establishment of Republican politics and capitalist philosophy should not be viewed as a surprise or a sudden capitulation. Rather, it reflected, in part, his need for a psychological respite, a retreat for his battle-scarred being; and it was an example of Jackie's continued independence of mind; he was a man who thought (and fought) for himself, *who valued and learned from his own personal experience.* This is crucial. If you read chapters 15, 16, 17 in *I Never Had It Made,* you get a thorough idea of how carefully Jackie considered his public and political options, and his political choices, including those as a black capitalist. For him it was not a matter of personal gain as much as it was a matter of opening doors to the big world of business and politics for his race. Once more Jackie was his own man, smart, tough, and independent, and it would cost him. (As when, as part owner of the Harlem bank, he had to turn out the black president he had helped select; once he saw that the man was corrupt and negligent, Jackie helped force him to resign; for this act of integrity he was criticized sharply by some of his own people, which stabbed Jackie in a new way.)

The hurt and injury, and the new assaults (or betrayals), would continue. In 1967, just twenty years after his pioneering work in

transforming baseball and the nation, after his singular breakthrough success, a new crop of young black militants accused him
of being an "Uncle Tom," created by white people, for his pro-
business, pro-Rockefeller allegiances. A cruel irony, this backstab-
bing. (Perhaps like certain Jews accusing Louis Brandeis of selling
out by joining the Supreme Court and not sticking with the Zionist movement.) While the country had moved gradually forward,
the new black militants were impatient and angry; they were
attempting to change black consciousness, and in the process chal-
lenging the old Negro heroes. In the November 30, 1963, *Amsterdam News,* Malcolm X wrote an "Open Letter" to Jackie, attacking
him viciously for his succession of white bosses, for whom he was
still "trying to win The Big Game," and for misleading African
Americans in the Robeson incident, supporting temporarily the
Nixon campaign, and now the Rockefeller connection. Robinson
never showed the proper appreciation for the "support given him
by the Negro masses." And somewhat later, Amiri Baraki (the
playwright Leroi Jones), in *The Autobiography of Leroi Jones*
(1984), went after Jackie with equal virulence, calling him "a syn-
thetic colored guy," who was "imperfected" at the California labo-
ratories of USC" (wrong school!), whose "ersatz blackness" could
represent the shadow of the Negro integrating into America."
Such were the rewards for Jackie, in his late life, for being a gutsy
pioneer, a valiant black Moses, an American hero. (Fortunately,
Negroes around the country knew Jackie far better than those
young Turks, and felt a little differently, as did Martin Luther
King, who in 1968 saluted him, saying that he would not be where
he was without standing on the shoulders of Jackie Robinson.)

Still, Jackie did not back off the battle with his young attack-
ers. Jackie knew his own experience well, and trusted its wisdom.
He who had never backed down with nasty white racists would

not back down now with mischievous black radicals. Here is a letter he wrote to Malcolm X, responding to his cheap charges:

> *I am proud of my association with the men you chose to call my "white bosses." I am also proud that so many others whom you would undoubtedly label as "white bosses," marched with us to Washington and have been and are now working with our leaders to help achieve equality in America.*
>
> *I will not dignify your attempted slur against my appearance before the House Un-American Committee some years back. All I can say is that if I were called upon to defend my country today, I would gladly do so. Nor do I hide behind any coat-tails as you do when caught in one of your numerous outlandish statements. Your usual "out" is to duck responsibility by stating: "The Honorable Elijah Muhammad says . . ."*
>
> *Personally I reject your racist views. I reject your dream of a separate state.*
>
> *I do not do things to please "white bosses" or "black agitators" unless they are things which please me. You say I have never shown appreciation to the Negro masses. I assume that is why NAACP branches all over the country constantly invite me to address them and this is the reason the NAACP gave me the highest award, the Spingarn Medal.*
>
> *You mouth a big and bitter battle, Malcolm, but it is noticeable that your militancy is mainly expressed in Harlem where it is safe. I have always contended for your right—as for that of every American—to say and think and believe what you choose. I just happen to believe you*

*are supporting and advocating policies which could not
possibly interest the masses. Thank God for our Dr. Bunche,
our Roy Wilkins, our Dr. King and our Mr. Randolph.*

How tough, forthright, and critical a response! Jackie was never
one to mince words or, as we have seen, to back away from a battle,
be it against a bigoted player, a bigoted manager or Army sergeant,
or now a black racist. He spoke his mind, in columns, talks, and
letters. We admired him so much for this honesty and gutsiness, as
we always had. If he thought the path toward social betterment
for fellow Negroes was via the economic power provided by capitalist enterprise and entrepreneurship (à la Marcus Garvey), such
as business ventures and bank creations, he proved to be way ahead
of his time, years before fellows like Bill Cosby and Robert L.
Johnson. (Moreover, looking ahead a few decades into the future,
it is worth noting who would come to write laudatory introduc-
tions to new editions of Jackie's autobiographies; it was black
spokesmen as diverse as Spike Lee and Cornel West, not to mention the great Hank Aaron. For those and other leading black
figures, Jackie remained their original hero, The Man Who
Opened—or Broke Down—the Door.

(It should be said that while Joe Louis had been a major hero
in the 1940s—especially after his "patriotic" knockout victory
over Max Schmeling in 1938—his sport had already been open to
Negroes, and also, boxing was not nearly as popular as the national
pastime, baseball. Jack had met Joe in 1942, when both were in
Army training camp in Fort Riley, Kansas, and though they
couldn't be more unlike each other, they became good friends,
golfing and riding horses together. Jackie later said that Louis's
popularity had paved the way for Jackie to break down baseball's
racial barrier. A gentlemanly compliment from one great to
another great.)

We should remember that, during these difficult "citizen" years, Jackie had no baseball field to take out his frustrations on, no opposing team to defeat and scourge, no green fields for pleasure and relief, and for ravishing revenge. The baseball diamond was gone. It was like taking away the blank pages and pens from Thoreau and Emerson, and asking them to survive and do battle in their final years without being able to write down their moral thoughts and ideas. No more influential essays. Wouldn't have been easy. And it was not fun for us to watch Jackie in the final years, a graying ghost of a man, immersed in arguments, speeches, and heated politics, moving slowly, growing paunchy—a far cry from running the dirt base paths on green fields and startling us with his bravado steals and provocative leads. The shift to civilian garb and more prosaic doings was dramatic, pointed, poignant.

But of course we still memorialized him, loved him, and still worshipped the myth, since the man now was a different person. Or he wore a different mask and costume, and walked—or hobbled—with a different gait. But for most of us, he could still do little wrong, and it was almost as if time had stood still, frozen back in the late forties and fifties, when the Bums were still in Brooklyn and Jackie was still the passionate leader. I think the borough lived by way of that myth, was still stoked by that passion, and did not yet allow itself, post-1957, to understand or accept that it was the end of the day, the end of the old town and its beliefs. When we saw Jackie now on the television or in the news, we were viewing a kind of montage, I think, one image that of the gray-haired lumbering suit and, superimposed upon that, the image of the youthful, fiery baser runner. Maybe it was that Robinson had given us such pleasure that we couldn't get over him, or didn't want to? The philosopher Kierkegaard wrote, "Most men pursue pleasure with such breathless haste that they hurry past it." We in Brooklyn didn't want to hurry past it, even though it was a decade or more old, and even though our old baseball god had disappeared. That pleasure lingered with us, so strong was its aroma and power, and lingers still for me *six decades later.*

If the baseball field was gone for Jackie, so was his older friend, beloved boss, and wise counselor. In December of 1965 Branch Rickey had died at age eighty-three, and this left a definite void, once filled with comfort and compassion, in Jack's life. When few blacks attended Rickey's funeral, in Ohio, Jackie was openly angry, and he criticized black athletes. "Not even flowers or telegrams, and they're earning all that money," he said. Monte Irving thought that many of the players had come to associate the arrogance of Jackie with Mr. Rickey, and that is why they stayed away. But Campanella, who couldn't come, still confined to a wheelchair from his tragic car accident, maintained his huge warm feelings toward Mr. Rickey. "He made me a better catcher, a better person on and off the field. He made me a completely changed individual." Robinson was broken-hearted, even though he hadn't seen his old friend in a while. "The passing of Mr. Rickey is like losing a father," said Jackie. "My wife and I feel like we've lost someone very dear to us. Mr. Rickey's death is a great loss not only to baseball but to America. His life was full, and I'm sure there are no regrets as far as fulfillment in life. I think he did it all." The shrewd and valiant older man who had first taken up the great challenge, and the father figure who had then nurtured the young lad throughout his major league career, and ordeal, was gone. And Jackie felt it deeply, and suffered. Another fateful blow.

And this fan, then a graduate student in California, mourned the passing too, and took out his old childhood scrapbook with the pasted-in photos and looked through the iconic photos, one of Jackie and Mr. Rickey shaking hands at the first signing, another of Rickey working at his desk, in his bow tie and eyeglasses looking like FDR; and an early one of him as a young coach of the Ohio Wesleyan baseball team in tie and broad-brimmed hat, looking like a Methodist preacher. What a citizen, what a gentleman, and what a lover of baseball.

Once again, a new twist: while he was assaulted by the young Turks, Jackie surprised and angered the Negro establishment when he tossed away his membership in the NAACP, where he had long been a leading spokesman, precisely because it was dominated by a "clique of the Old Guard" who had failed to include "younger, more progressive voices." What a surprising irony. For here was Jackie, *squeezed on both sides by his own people,* a public figure beset with new contradictions and new pressures. Baseball probably looked a lot easier, felt more idyllic—Ebbets Field, his old playground for having fun and releasing pressures, was gone, like his youthful body—than being a political figure on a formal national stage, pulled this way and tugged that way, with no chance to run, steal a base, or agitate a pitcher. Missing now were the exuberant pleasures of boyhood and youth, the salad days of sporting competition in which he could physically work through anxieties and forget tensions and come out ahead, constantly supported and cheered on by a crowd of Brooklyn faithful who had come to watch and worship him.

This post-baseball Jackie was in a new uncharted territory of big-time politicians and black power advocates, corporate leaders and media commentators, with a very different audience of non-baseball people, where public posturing and political rhetoric counted. No playing field with clear rules and appointed umpires and final scores in this arena. And no trusted, avuncular Prospero Rickey to look after his special Caliban. The results now produced no clear outcome, no final score; and for Jackie the political player, this was new, confusing, and strange. The fiery look in his eyes was gone, physically and spiritually, as old friends noted. (Among them were baseball writers like Lester Rodney and Wendell Smith, Sam Lacy and Roger Kahn, and friends and teammates like Reese and Newcombe and Campanella.) Further, the fire in his heart was now almost out, down to ashes. The twin forces competing in his heart, W. E. B. Du Bois versus Booker T. Washington, had dissipated, and what was left was a pale version of each. What could drive him now?

Consider Sonnet 73 of Shakespeare as a fitting elegy for Jack's last years:

> *That time of year thou mayst in me behold*
> *When yellow leaves, or none, or few, do hang*
> *Upon those boughs which shake against the cold,*
> *Bare ruin'd choirs, where late the sweet birds sang.*
> *In me thou seest the twilight of such day*
> *As after sunset fadeth in the west;*
> *Which by and by black night doth take away,*
> *Death's second self, that seals up all in rest.*
> *In me thou seest the glowing of such fire,*
> *That on the ashes of his youth doth lie,*
> *As the death-bed, whereon it must expire,*
> *Consumed with that which it was nourish'd by.*
> > *This thou perceiv'st, which makes thy love more strong,*
> > *To love that well which thou must leave ere long.*

If Jackie had lost his youth, his health, his looks, his joy, Brooklyn had lost its Jackie, its team, its bliss—meaning its deep faith and its high religion: Dodgers baseball. Truthfully, this loss had taken its toll on the devoted borough and its three million fans.

The godlike Bums, exemplified by the teams that Jackie had played and starred on, from 1947 to 1953, had been transferred— or exiled—to Los Angeles in 1957. The sacred Ebbets Field was torn down in 1960 and made into apartment buildings; would the French tear down its Notre Dame Cathedral or the English its Tower of London? The result was a loss of shaman-power and city-soul for the charming town ("Breucklyn," old Dutch village), and a diminution of its magical status. No longer was the subway ride across the river to our Brooklyn a Canterbury-like religious site to be visited by devoted pilgrims of baseball from all over the country. And no more was Jackie the brilliant galloping spirit spearheading the club in exciting games and lifting the town to a state of sustained exultant celebration. Those days were finished. All the community meetings and Robert Moses promises and mayoral plans to try to reinvent the Dodgers and Ebbets Field on home turf produced no results. Brooklyn after 1957 was never the same, its vital soul, created by Jackie, tarnished, *its people left without a great religious and sporting site to gather at, mingle, worship.*

So Jackie in his last years did not have the blue and white flannel to protect and shield him, or have any longer his adoring audience, or the sport he loved, or the baseball club that honored and knighted him. Or his mother, Mallie, who had died in 1968, three years after the death of Mr. Rickey. Little wonder that he had turned down O'Malley and Los Angeles, for he was tethered emotionally to us, in Brooklyn. He was on his own—except for Rachel of course—bereft and increasingly ill. The tragic arc of the last years continued, and while he wore the medals of the former service, he was a civilian now—a public spokesman in the service of Rockefeller Republican interests and civil rights, but in his heart an injured, baffled, and perhaps underappreciated, black man. A bundle of tormenting conditions and contradictions.

And yet, during those late, sad, semi-tragic years, there were also moments and occasions of high glory, new recognition. At a gala political affair in a crowded New York City ballroom, for example, as he chatted with a few people Jackie was interrupted by a balding fellow in a tuxedo who had walked across the floor to salute him; the elderly gentleman turned out to be President Dwight Eisenhower. ("I couldn't believe it," Jackie told friend Mal Goode, "The President did it because he wanted to shake my hand.") In December 1971, at the twenty-fifth anniversary of *Sport* magazine at Mama Leone's Restaurant in New York, Jack was honored along with the greatest figures in sports, among them Arnold Palmer, Bill Russell, Rocky Marciano, Gale Sayers, Rod Laver, Johnny Unitas, and Gordie Howe. Of all these sports giants, it was Jackie who was selected as "The Man of 25 Years in Sports." If you consider that list, this was maybe his most impressive honor.

And most importantly, five years after his retirement from the game, in his very first year of eligibility, 1962, he was inducted into the Baseball Hall of Fame. The plaque in Cooperstown reads:

JACK ROOSEVELT ROBINSON, BROOKLYN N. L. 1947–1956
LEADING NL BATTER IN 1949. HOLDS FIELDING MARK
FOR SECOND BASEMAN PLAYING 150 OR MORE GAMES WITH
.992. LEAD N. L. IN STOLEN BASES IN 1947 AND 1949.
MOST VALUABLE PLAYER IN 1949. LIFETIME BATTING
AVERAGE .311. JOINT RECORD HOLDER FOR MOST DOUBLE
PLAYS BY SECOND BASEMAN, 137 IN 1951. LED SECOND
BASEMEN IN DOUBLE PLAYS 1949–50–51–52.

Jackie called up three people to stand at his side for the Cooperstown ceremony: his mother, Mallie; his wife, Rachel; his mentor, Branch Rickey. Thus Jackie became the first Negro player ever to enter the Baseball Hall of Fame. I was a graduate student at Stanford when this occurred, and I thought, He did it again: the pioneer kid from Pasadena has broken down yet another major wall. Few of my friends felt the moment the way I did, as I walked across the Spanish tile quad. From then on, blacks in the future, as well as Negroes from the past, were allowed entry into the oldest and most sacred of the sports halls of fame.

The noted baseball analyst Bill James ranked Jackie, in his peak years, second all-time to Joe Morgan as a second baseman, while admitting that he hadn't seen Jackie play, and that maybe he could have been first. He said, "It could be that the greatest second baseman ever was Jackie Robinson, but for me to say that just places too much of a load on intangibles that I didn't see and that I couldn't specifically identify" (*Historical Baseball Abstract*). This honesty is commendable. But I did see them both play, and I would reverse that order, putting Jackie up there at the top. Those intangibles were significant, from his skills at bunting and running the bases, to intimidating the opposing pitchers and catchers when on the bases, to his clutch playing and ability to win in a variety of ways. And who can measure, as I said earlier, the on-base intimidation factor for the pitcher and current hitter? (Like Ruth at bat, say, intimidating the pitcher for the hitter before or after him.) Not to mention the tremendous excitement that Jackie created, in a sport of quiet routine for the most part, every time he stepped onto the field. The astonishing thing was that Jackie's professional career lasted only ten years, since he wasn't a rookie until age twenty-seven. Had he begun earlier, at twenty-two or twenty-three, as Campanella had mentioned—when no colored player was allowed to play in the major leagues—he would have broken most if not all of the statistical records.

But Jackie's game was not about statistics, the measurement by which most baseball journalists and media evaluators seem to judge the game. It was about his subtle skills, his game intelligence, his spirit, his cunning, his adventurousness, his clutch play. He created a style of play all his own, which was aggressive, provocative, and native-lyrical, if it may be described that way, something akin to a uniquely lyrical literary voice, like that of Saul Bellow. The aesthetic pleasures of that singular style were tangible, and they produced game results. That's what you remember about his play, the sheer pleasure he—and it—gave you. It was a combination of entertainment, professionalism, and excellence of an elegant sort—the deft slides, the taking of the extra base, the tantalizing leads, the exquisite torture of the pitcher and catcher. There has been no one like him in the last sixty years—though "The Say Hey Kid" Willie Mays in center field came close, in skills and athletic aesthetics—and for that reason alone, he was a very special player, one who flashed poetry in his unorthodox running, fulfilled and exceeded expectations in the clutch, and forever was creating beauty in his all-around play.

To celebrate Jackie's induction into the Hall of Fame, a huge party for about nine hundred was thrown in his honor at the Waldorf Astoria, organized by Dr. King and hosted by Governor Rockefeller of New York, who called Jackie "a hero of the struggle to make American democracy a genuine reality for every American." High tributes came in from many, including two presidents, Richard Nixon and John F. Kennedy. But the most important one perhaps came from Martin Luther King, who hailed Jackie's achievements and defended his right to speak out on all matters pertaining to segregation, civil rights, and politics. "He has the right, because back in the days when integration wasn't fashionable, he underwent the trauma and the humiliation and the loneliness which comes with being a pilgrim walking the lonesome byways toward the high road of Freedom. He was a sit-inner before sit-ins, a freedom rider before freedom rides. And that is why we honor him tonight." Dr. King sent this tribute from Albany, Georgia, about ninety miles from where Robinson was born on a plantation in 1919, while King was enmeshed in a crisis in the civil rights movement as it confronted one of the major centers of segregation.

Great as his baseball accomplishments were that led him into the HOF and justified high praise at the gala event, something Jackie did a little while before the event was also worthy of praise. A real estate controversy had developed up in Harlem, involving a white (Jewish) owner named Singer of a chain steak restaurant about to open and a Negro owner of an already-existing steakhouse, and when Lewis H. Michaux, president of a black nationalist group, entered the fray, suddenly the issue flared into virulent anti-Semitism. Protestors held up placards and chanted, "Jew go away—black man stay!" and vilified Singer and Frank Schiffman, the popular owner of the Apollo Theater, as "The Merchant of Venice" (Rampersad). Inserting his usual intrepid will, Jackie countered with a column for the *Amsterdam News*, decrying the anti-Jewish rhetoric of Michaux's supporters and asserting, "Anti-Semitism is as rotten as anti-Negroism. It is a shame that, so far, none of the Negroes of Harlem have yet had the guts to say so in tones which could be heard throughout the city." Once again Jackie was being Jackie, never ducking a battle or a problem that he might have avoided. For this he was attacked in a "hate Jackie Robinson campaign" ("Old Black Joe—Jackie must go."). But he was backed strongly by the likes of Roy Wilkens, A. Philip Randolph, Whitney Young, Ralph Bunche, and old friend Reverend George Lawrence of the Antioch Baptist Church in Brooklyn, who wrote to support Jackie's "magnificent stand against anti-

Semitism." In the end full peace was made, the bigotry ceased, and both Schiffman and Michaux sat at the same Waldorf table honoring Jackie.

But for me personally, his best support came from my estranged father, who used the occasion to send along a few clippings and a note to me at Stanford: "Well you should see what your Robinson *bucher* did up in Harlem. Read his column. *Ken-a-horah*, he's not just a ballplayer but a real mensch." This reconnection with my father, via Jackie, and that special Yiddish noun of affirmation for the kind of man Jackie was, touched me. Harry had become a full convert, and was trying to become a full father.

Then he added, in a memorable postscript: "You remember Moishe from the Sutter Avenue Deli? Well a while ago we were kibbitzing, and he was amazed that I had known and followed Jackie Robinson. '*You*, Hershel, *of all people? You know what, you've finally become a real American citizen!' Funny, eh, sonnyboy?*"

For different reasons, I was terribly moved.

Losing the Dodgers, losing Jackie, meant more than was apparent, for they were symbolic entities as much as concrete realities. They represented so much: emotion, pleasure, prestige, patriotism, devotion. Our Brooklyn, once an appendage of Manhattan, known for its unique suspension Bridge and Coney Island steeplechase, and for Whitman poetry and Gershwin jazz, became known nationwide for its stylish baseball team and its defiant ebony hero. (Maybe a little like Pushkin and Moscow?) Ebbets Field was the site where the biggest event for Negroes probably since the emancipation had taken place, and where the question of race was being tested daily in our national pastime game. We the fans, especially the kids, had become one with the team and one with Jackie, an identity forged by new openness, underdog passion, fantastic victories. An identity created by a new diversity. Put another way, perhaps too simply, what Whitman had started, Jackie had completed. And all of it was snatched from us by an insider thief in the middle of the night, while public officials stood by and watched it all, in shock and disbelief. It was like having your family taken away one night, while you slept, and when you awoke, you were told that they were taken to some faraway land never to return. And it was all legal. So that you were condemned to live with their memory, vivid and precise in all details and levels, while you grew up as an orphan.

A few pages ago I cited Shakespeare's Sonnet 73, as an elegy for the latter-day Jackie. Earlier on, in my *Brooklyn Boy*, I wrote my own sort of ode, in prose, for the city.

In a section called "The Bridge," I wrote about the history of that iconic symbol, designed by Roebling and opened in 1883, the first great suspension bridge, and what it meant to me as a youth, about age fifteen or so, when I first walked across it. It felt like walking through a giant erector set, with the slope of steel cables arching way above me, all held together with bolts and rivets, for a river span of 1,595 feet, with a total length of some 6,000 feet. What a fantasy walk, in the evening especially, with the bright stars and constellations shining. Viewing the lit vertical colossus of Manhattan in the distance as I marched toward that glittering destination, I had a double sense, you could say: of the solidity of the home ground, and the necessity of departing to explore the larger world beyond. For once in that world, I felt I could measure properly my own experience of coming of age in Brooklyn. Yet even when you left, I sensed, and learned, you didn't leave; you took some visiting tours outside.

And naturally, at the end of the two-hour-plus walk, when I looked back I saw that smaller waterfront and that cozy turf of my childhood and youth, which would hover in my memory. I recalled all those curious Dutch names for the very first six villages settled, some three hundred years before: Breuckelen, Midwout, Gravesend, Nieuw Utrecht, Bushwick, Amersfoort (Flatlands)—for me, sites of high school fields and gyms as much as neighborhoods. Brooklyn made inward sense as much as outward. So it seemed clear to me that that fabled bridge led to the past as much as to the future. As much a bridge of dreams then, a spur to suspension of disbelief, as a great suspension bridge.

In describing all that in my autobiographical novel, I felt the power of that bridge in the same way I felt the power of Jackie, as real and as metaphysical, a force of steel and a force of dreams, both dramatizing my feelings for Brooklyn.

At the Riverfront Stadium in Cincinnati in October 1972, Jackie threw out the first ball in the second game of the World Series. A fan brought up a baseball for him to sign, but Jackie told him he couldn't see it, and he didn't want to mess up any of the other signatures on the ball; the fan told him his was the only autograph he wanted. A few minutes later, on national television, he pronounced, "I'd like to live to see a black manager. I'd like to live to see a black man coaching at third base." That political message, delivered during an honorific moment, irked and displeased some, but this was Jackie, outspoken and defiant to the last, a supporter of his people and equal justice until the very end. Physically depleted, in danger of having his legs amputated, his vision impaired, he remained his own man, and spiritually strong. The end came sooner than anyone expected, nine days later, on October 24, 1972. Jackie collapsed in his Stamford home, and was rushed to the hospital by a fire department ambulance. His heart had failed, and he died there, at age fifty-three. (He had promised Rockefeller he would give a speech for him in Albany, and although he knew he was bleeding beneath his eyes from the diabetes, and Rachel had advised him not to go, he insisted, saying he had made a commitment.)

The common folk of Harlem were able to view him first, at Duncan Brothers Funeral Home at Seventh Avenue and 135th Streets, but the official funeral was held on Friday, October 27, at noon in Riverside Church. A congregation of some twenty-five hundred filled the famed Gothic church, and among them were three daughters and a grandson of Branch Rickey, Roy Campanella in a wheelchair, Willie Mays, Monte Irvin, Hank Aaron, Hank Greenburg, Joe Louis, Governor Nelson Rockefeller, and baseball commissioner Bowie Kuhn. President Nixon sent a forty-man delegation to honor Robinson. The Reverend Jesse Jackson, whom Jackie had befriended, stood near the silver-blue coffin draped with flowers and delivered the eulogy. "When Jackie took the field, something reminded us of our birthright to be free." He went on, with baseball metaphors, speaking to the likes of civil rights leaders Roy Wilkins, A. Philip Randolph, and Bayard Rustin; singer Roberta Flack and political figure Sargent Shriver; Ed Sullivan and baseball executives Bill Veeck, Warren Giles, Peter O'Malley. The pallbearers were teammates Pee Wee Reese, Ralph Branca, Junior Gilliam, Don Newcombe, as well as Cleveland's Larry Doby, and Bill Russell, the basketball great. The funeral cortege moved gradually through the streets of Harlem and Bedford-Stuyvesant where tens of thousands lined the route and bid their farewell. Jackie was buried in Cypress Hills Cemetery, Brooklyn, a few miles from where he ran the bases and excited us in the old Ebbets Field, now the apartment complex.

I was teaching at Brandeis at the time, and when the news reached me I recall going down the leafy hillside into the Three Chapels area, and sitting down in the Berlin Chapel. It was empty in the late afternoon on a Tuesday. Two floor-to-ceiling windows in the small chapel let the light stream in, giving the pewter-colored walls a subtle sheen. I sat on a wooden bench in the narrow silent chapel. I thought back to Jackie's opening days when I was a boy of nine, first seeing him come onto the field, with his shining ebony skin, with Burt at my side. I was sorry Burt was not around any longer to be there with me, in his Air Force uniform, to remember the day and the special rookie. Who could have imagined that what we had witnessed, in April 1947, some fifty or sixty feet away on that cozy green field, would move outward, beyond the field and beyond Brooklyn, to sweep the country? And to change Brooklyn and our national history. Jackie's journey had been long and striking, from Pasadena playgrounds, to UCLA fields and track, to Delorimier Stadium (Montreal), to Ebbets Field; from a small athletic boy and athletic college youth, to a big-time star in the major leagues, to a major player in race and justice in the nation. One man, one baseball player. Long, arduous, and historic.

And for me, personally, it was a journey of memory, and understanding, of the broad-shouldered fellow in tan raincoat and the intense player in white and blue uniform, of his sober words and vivid presence; memories that stayed with me, drove me. There in that haunting chapel—the Berlin Chapel which resonated with the presence of all the Jewish (and other) immigrants he had inspired and drawn to baseball—I recalled many of those moments and scenes on the bright green diamond, such as his rising up from a successful steal of home plate, uniform dirtied, and walking pigeon-toed and almost painfully to the dugout where Pee Wee alone stood to greet him. Long blissful afternoons of childhood and youth, in the passionate company of a youthful hero; that was the way I would remember him throughout my life.

I stood up, and in the late afternoon light, seeing the autumnal trees beyond, I understood how lucky I had been. How lucky Brooklyn had been.

In the years since his death in 1972, Jackie has risen even more to full legendary status. (Indeed, a Hollywood movie, *42*, has been made—a highly romanticized version of the Jackie story, and while it hardly does justice to the real struggle or the true complexity of Jackie, it does commemorate the legend.) In the game of baseball, his number, 42, is now retired officially—no team can give it out to a player—and he is honored in every major league ball field, showing up on scoreboards and grandstands. Once every year or two there is a Jackie Robinson day at an All-Star Game or World Series. At various Hall of Fame ceremonies, a new inductee will invoke Jackie's name as the player who most inspired him. In the larger world of the Republic, President Reagan in March 1984 awarded him posthumously the highest civilian honor, the Medal of Freedom. In 1996 both houses of Congress authorized the minting of gold and silver coins of the realm commemorating the fiftieth anniversary of Jackie entering the major leagues in 1947; it was signed into law by President Clinton. There have been hundreds of significant testimonials, including those from Martin Luther King and President Barack Obama. Serious American historians have written about his accomplishments. Important black leaders and celebrities, from Bill Cosby to Martin Rustin, Sidney Poitier to Barack Obama, have remembered him and his imprint. My own teacher at Brooklyn College, the eminent historian John Hope Franklin, once told me that he considered Jackie the most significant Negro in America, in terms of his impact, before Martin Luther King. In an introduction to *Baseball Has Done It*, one of Jackie's autobiographies, Spike Lee writes, "As far back as I can remember, Jackie Robinson has been an inspiration in my life." And Cornel West has written, "More even than Abraham Lincoln and the Civil War, or Martin Luther King Jr. and the Civil Rights Movement, Jackie Robinson graphically symbolized and personified the challenge to the vicious legacy and ideology of white supremacy in American history." Some high praise, to be sure. Though not always duly remembered by contemporary black athletes—a shocking fact as Spike Lee has noted—Jackie has nevertheless been remembered and saluted by the most prominent members of the black community and by the baseball community.

In a society that takes its sports heroes very seriously, Jackie is up there with other icons like Babe Ruth and Joe DiMaggio and Willie Mays, Joe Louis and Jesse Owens, Michael Jordan and Bill Russell. Probably, along with The Babe (Ruth), Jackie stands at the top of the baseball list for immediate name recognition and sport association. But Jackie went beyond the sport. He moved into American history, into the *making* of our history. By following and excelling within the baseball rules, he created a new code of baseball ethics, and, by extension, he created a new ordering of the nation's moral codes. Yes, all that. Simultaneously he created, for many of us, a new layer of love and appreciation for the game by the way he played, something like a breakthrough novel—say, *Ulysses* by Joyce—that opens up the fullest possibilities of the genre. To my mind, Jackie opened up the baseball genre.

Of course, you don't see all those abstract virtues when you are a boy watching him play; rather you see only his wily anticipation on the base paths, the bravado of his steals, the smoothness of his double plays, the clutch hits and fielding gems, and the triumphs produced from his cunning gambles. You see how his is a beautiful game, in our one elegant sport, and it may be our curious fate— blessed or cursed?—that history will always come in second place to all that sporting excellence. Such is the nature of our country where Ruth may be as well known as Washington, and Jackie as Jefferson. Politics may rule the practical realm of adult power in our republic, but sports rules the the strongest fantasies and hopes of youth, both in rural and city life, and where, later, in our adult consciousness, it lingers as dreams in a subtle weave of longing, elegy and desire.

"If you take stock in souls," as Huck Finn says, "then you can't distinguish between their colors, because souls have no colors." Jackie did much—as much as anyone ever did in America—to prove that true, and to dramatize, by means of a game, our game, that colossal truth to a nation.

Bibliographical Note

O f the multitude of books on the subject, let me cite two that are essential reading. There is the exhaustive and excellent biography by Arnold Rampersad, *Jackie Robinson* (1997). And the historian Jules Tygiel has written an incisive social history of Jackie and the period, *Baseball's Great Experiment* (1997).

I want also to acknowledge the autobiographies written by Jackie, with the help of various sports writers: *Jackie Robinson: My Own Story* (1948), *Baseball Has Done It* (1964), *Breakthrough to the Big Leagues* (1965), and *I Never Had It Made* (1974). Jackie the writer, like the man, was insightful, frank, and always unafraid to speak his mind.

About the Author

Alan Lelchuk was born and raised in Brooklyn, attended public schools and Brooklyn College for his BA (1960) in World Literature and Stanford University for his graduate degrees in English (Ph.D. 1965). He began teaching at Brandeis in 1966–81, and since then, has been Visiting Writer at Amherst College, CCNY, Univ of Naples, The Free University in Berlin, and Moscow Sate University. In 2001–2002 he was the Salgo Professor of American literature and Writing at ELTE in Budapest. He has been the recipient of Guggenheim and Fulbright Awards for fiction, and a residency in Mishkenot Sha'Ananim. His novels include American Mischief, Miriam at Thirty-four, Shrinking: The Beginning of My Own Ending, Miriam In Her Forties, "On Home Ground' (for young adults), Brooklyn Boy, Playing the Game, Ziff: A Life? and most recently, "Searching for Wallenberg."

He has co-edited (in English) "8 Great Hebrew Short Novels," was Associate Editor of Modern Occasions (with Philip Rahv), and a co-founder of Steerforth Press.

He has been on the Dartmouth College faculty since 1985, lives in Canaan, New Hampshire, is married, and has two grown sons.